The Lesser Evil?

The Lesser Evil?

Debates on the Democratic Party and
Independent Working-Class Politics

Jack Barnes ■ Stanley Aronowitz
Peter Camejo ■ Michael Harrington
George Breitman ■ Carl Haessler

Pathfinder
New York ■ London ■ Montreal ■ Sydney

Edited by Duncan Williams

Copyright © 1977 by Pathfinder Press
All rights reserved

ISBN 978-0-87348-518-0
Library of Congress Catalog Card Number 77-85124
Manufactured in Canada

First edition, 1977
Eighth printing, 2021

Pathfinder
www.pathfinderpress.com
E-mail: pathfinder@pathfinderpress.com

Contents

Preface 7

On the participants 9

Is Carter the lesser evil?
Michael Harrington vs. Peter Camejo (1976) 11

What is the Democratic Party coalition?
Jack Barnes vs. Stanley Aronowitz (1965) 57

Should progressives work in the Democratic Party?
Carl Haessler vs. George Breitman (1959) 119

Index 153

Preface

For several generations, American politics has been defined by the two-party system, with a few short-lived exceptions. The capitalist Democratic and Republican parties have monopolized political life and attempted to force dissent into channels acceptable to the ruling rich. It has long been argued that while the Democratic Party is not fundamentally different from the Republican Party, it offers a worthwhile arena where advocates of labor, democratic rights, racial justice, women's rights, and general social progress can present their programs; while still undemocratic and unrepresentative, the Democratic Party represents a "lesser evil" than the Republicans.

The three debates in this book, held in 1976, 1965, and 1959, all address this problem: Is it worthwhile for people who consider themselves progressives, radicals, even socialists, to work in and support the Democratic Party? In each case, the negative is argued by a member of the Socialist Workers Party; the positive is argued by radicals of different shades of opinion. Notes on the participants are provided on p. 9.

The debate format is suitable for a book whose purpose is to illustrate the counterposition of ideas as applied to immediate political experiences. Unnecessary repetition has been eliminated, and some passages have been edited to help the reader follow the line of argument, but in all cases we have tried to make the printed text correspond to the speeches as they were given. Except where the meaning would have been unclear, grammar and syntax have been left as in the spoken version.

Because the debates were held before audiences whose members shared a knowledge of contemporary and local history, some events and people are referred to with no explanation. In notes preceding each debate, we have attempted to fill in some of the information that might help the reader with such references.

On the participants

Jack Barnes (b. 1940) is national secretary of the Socialist Workers Party. In 1965, at the time of the debate published here, he was national chairman of the Young Socialist Alliance. He is the author of *The Changing Face of U.S. Politics: Working-Class Politics and the Trade Unions*, and of numerous articles in *New International*, a magazine of Marxist politics and theory.

Stanley Aronowitz (b. 1933) was, at the time of the 1965 debate, a leader of Students for a Democratic Society and the Committee for Independent Political Action in New York City, and an editor of the magazine *Studies on the Left*.

✻

Carl Haessler (1888–1972) was, at the time of the 1959 debate, a member of the Socialist Party who had been imprisoned for opposing World War I.

George Breitman (1916–1986) was, at the time of the 1959 debate, a leader of the Socialist Workers Party in Detroit, Michigan, and a frequent writer for the *Militant*, a socialist newsweekly.

✻

Michael Harrington (1928–1989) was, at the time of the 1976 debate, chairman of the Democratic Socialist Organizing

Committee (now the Democratic Socialists of America) and a professor at Queens College in New York City.

Peter Camejo (1939–2008) was, at the time of the 1976 debate, the Socialist Workers Party candidate for president of the United States.

Is Carter the lesser evil?
Michael Harrington vs. Peter Camejo

The following debate was held at Queens College in New York City on November 1, 1976—one day before the election of Jimmy Carter. Peter Camejo and his Socialist Workers Party running mate, Willie Mae Reid, appearing on the ballot in twenty-eight states, received more than 90,000 votes.

Because of the location of the debate, the New York City budget crisis was a focus of discussion. The cutbacks closed down or curtailed the operations of child-care centers, hospitals, schools, libraries, and other municipal social services; eliminated 50,000 city jobs; and ended free tuition and open admissions in the City University of New York system.

In spite of this attack on the workers' living standards, there was no change in the political strategy of the leaders of the large New York union movement. All of them, including Social Democrats such as Victor Gotbaum, head of District Council 37 of the American Federation of State, County and Municipal Employees (AFSCME), had supported Democrat Abraham Beame for mayor in 1973 and Democrat Hugh Carey for governor in 1974. While Beame and Carey carried through the cutbacks, the union leaders had nothing to recommend but the election of Democrat Carter in 1976.

The debate first appeared in the November 26, December 3, and December 10, 1976, issues of the socialist weekly, the *Militant*.

Is Carter the lesser evil?

PRESENTATIONS

MICHAEL HARRINGTON: First of all, I'd like to begin by specifying what we're debating. We're not debating whether the United States needs political change much more radical than anything Jimmy Carter offers. Of course it does. It needs a restructuring of a society in which the government consistently follows corporate priorities to antisocial consequence. It needs, ultimately—both in terms of the nation and the world—democratic socialism. We are not debating the desirability of that.

We are not, as far as I am concerned, debating whether or not the Democratic Party is a party filled with contradictions, containing corporate interests, racists, etc. Of course it is.

We are not debating whether or not it is desirable to have a party realignment and to bring the millions of people—perhaps 50 percent of the electorate—who are excluded from this election into the political process. Of course we want to do that.

The question is not whether America needs radical change. The question is not whether America needs a new political voice and current. The question is, *how do you get it?*

The Socialist Workers Party says you get that change by voting tomorrow for Peter Camejo for president of the United States.

I say, the Democratic Socialist Organizing Committee of which I am chairman says, that tomorrow you should vote for Jimmy Carter—without any illusions—because he is clearly and infinitely better than Gerald Ford, but not good enough. You therefore vote for him because he's better, without illusions because he's not good enough. And you seize your vote, you take your vote, not as a final and decisive act, but as the first stage in trying to make the transformation which this society desperately needs.

Let me try to develop that analysis in three different ways. First of all, by a brief historical-theoretical presentation of the case for my point of view. Second, by a consideration of the question: Is there no difference between Ford and Carter? And third, by asking you: What do you think the impact would be on the politics of social change if tomorrow Gerald Ford wins or if tomorrow Jimmy Carter wins? Which victory is not only better in and of itself, but is better from the point of view of energizing the millions of people in America who must be energized for much more basic change than they can vote for tomorrow?

So first of all, a historical-theoretical perspective. There was once a socialist political leader. He joined a workers' movement, the majority of whose members was not socialist. A workers' movement so confused that they elected an industrialist to the board of directors. A workers' movement so utterly confused that perhaps the majority of the workers in it were against the right to strike. A workers' movement that viewed the limitation of the working day to ten hours as a gigantic triumph. He joined that movement in spite of all those enormous limitations, because it was a movement of the working people; because it was a political movement of the working people. He did not require that it have the correct program. He went with the movement because he understood that only by going with the movement can you change the society and change the movement itself.

That man's name was, of course, Karl Marx. The movement I refer to was the International Workingmen's Association, the First International, the first international association of the socialist movement.

Karl Marx is dead. Karl Marx cannot tell me how to vote tomorrow. But he had an analysis, a point of view that I think permits me to confront situations that Karl Marx never dreamed of. And I want to be as radical as Marx was in the case of the First International. I want to go with workers in political movement because, like Marx, I believe that's where the possibility of change is.

I suggest to you that this election in a confused way, in a way which I have not invented, but in a very real way, is a counterposition of social classes.

Here is a class-conscious magazine. It's called *Fortune* magazine. It represents the class consciousness of the corporate rich in America. It tells us that the executives of the top 500 corporations in the United States are going to vote 85.2 percent for Gerald Ford; 10.4 percent for Jimmy Carter.

That class understands where its class interests lie. Corporate big business is not voting for Ford because they like his smile. They are voting for Ford because they know he will represent them.

Second, the labor movement in this country is supporting Carter. Now, the Socialist Workers Party in its various campaign analyses says that the workers should "think politically." The problem for the Socialist Workers Party is the workers *are* thinking politically. They're thinking Jimmy Carter.

They are thinking politically on an organized class basis. Tomorrow, class organizations of the workers, organizations you can join only by virtue of your membership in a union, are going to be mobilizing voters. If Carter wins, he will owe his victory in considerable measure to the working class politically organized as a class. That is a reality. One may not like this working class. One may wish it had other politics. I certainly do. But there is a working class in America. It is politically organized. It is for Carter. There is a corporate class. It is politically organized. It is for Ford.

There is in America tomorrow, if you will, a political class struggle taking place at the ballot box. And I suggest that from my point of view, I'm going to go where that workers' movement is and where that corporate movement is not.

Bertolt Brecht, after the East German general strike [in 1953], said something very nasty to the East German Stalinists who had pointed out the working class had not recognized its own class interests. Brecht said, "Why don't you dissolve this working class and invent a new one instead?" I'm afraid that's what the SWP is doing. In the name of the working class, they are counterposing themselves to the actual working class.

Moreover, the actual working class, although I don't agree with it on everything, is right that Carter is better for full employment, for national health, for tax reform, for all kinds of issues that affect our lives.

The SWP has a scenario. You can read it in their documents. That scenario: America is going to change, first by the victory of a class-struggle wing in the trade union movement which will totally transform the trade union movement. Secondly, the totally transformed trade union movement will become the basis of a political party. And that political party will become a revolutionary socialist party. *Do not hold your breath* for all that to happen.

In an America in which Gerald Ford is within a hair of

winning the presidency of the United States, to talk about revolutionary and cataclysmic possibilities, which is what the SWP does, is to talk, in my opinion, fantasy. Indeed, if we get the kind of cataclysmic change that the SWP talks about in its documents, I suspect that the beneficiary will not be a socialist movement on the left. If you get that kind of cataclysmic change, it is much more likely that the beneficiary will be a fascist movement of the right.

What I am saying is what we have to do is give up revolutionary fantasies and imaginary working classes and go where real workers are today organized politically. Not to accept what is wrong in their point of view, but to work with them because they will not trust you in talking about where they should go if you're counterposed to them.

Which leads me to the second point. Is there no difference between Ford and Carter? The SWP in its program has got some fine stuff: we have to get jobs for youths, Blacks, women, all kinds of things. Fine. Full employment is critical. You cannot solve a single problem in the United States without full employment. Is there no difference between Ford and Carter on full employment?

Carter is in favor of a bill guaranteeing the right to work to every worker in the United States. That bill's not half good enough. Carter is not half good enough for it. But he is for it and Ford is against it. We don't have to imagine. Ford vetoes job-generating bills. He's done it. He'll do it. Is there no difference? There's a difference to the more than seven million people who are unemployed in the United States. Ford wants them to be miserable because he sees no reason to do anything else. Carter wants to change their position.

Now, the SWP's answer to this is to basically repeat a point—the same point Senator Robert Dole makes—that war spending and mass murder abroad is the only Democratic Party formula for providing jobs. That's not true to begin with historically. It's not true because during the New

Deal, Roosevelt didn't create enough jobs, but Roosevelt created jobs before war spending took over in 1939, by public works. And Dole and the SWP can think it was only the war and simplify a complex case. The war obviously played an enormous role. But public service jobs did something. Kennedy and Johnson generated jobs before the war in Vietnam was escalated.

And I think it is terrible for left-wingers to make a right-wing point and try to miseducate the American people that either you go all the way to socialism or you can't do anything about unemployment short of a radical restructuring of society. The fact is you can. It has been done.

The fact is the struggle today for jobs is in the Democratic Party. It's around the Hawkins-Humphrey bill. It is supported by the working people. It is supported by the Black people and the other minorities in the United States. It is supported by the women's movement, or the best of the politically organized women's movement. There is a difference.

There is no difference between Ford and Carter on New York City? To state the proposition shows you how absurd it is. Ford wants us to drop dead. With Carter we've got a chance, not for justice, but to survive. Tell the kids in the public schools in New York City, tell the kids there is no difference. Tell the teachers. My son's in Public School 3 in Manhattan and we are seeing that school destroyed. And there is a possibility we can do something with a Carter victory. There is none with a Ford victory.

There is no difference to women? If Gerald Ford is elected president of the United States, he will continue the miserable, reactionary work in the Supreme Court that Richard Nixon began. And the Supreme Court, which has already been moved by Nixon's victory to the right, will move further to the right. And the Supreme Court is a crucial area for the women's movement in terms of the right to abortion as well as many other issues.

National health: there is no difference? Gerald Ford is up there with an absolute swindle, lying to the American people that a catastrophic health insurance is a national health program. Jimmy Carter is committed to the Kennedy-Corman national health program. You know who Carter's likely secretary of Health, Education and Welfare is? Leonard Woodcock, the president of the United Auto Workers, the principal trade union leader—along with George Meany—of a fight for national health in this country. You cannot say there is no difference.

On foreign policy. There is no difference between the greatest arms salesman in the world, Gerald Ford, and somebody who wants to curb it, Jimmy Carter? There is no difference when jobs has been one of the few issues Carter has raised in this campaign? And he raised the issue of nuclear proliferation. That makes a difference, not simply to America, but to all of mankind.

Which leads me to my final point. My final point is, what happens if Ford wins? What happens on Wednesday, November 3? If Ford wins, do you think the trade union movement is going to become more militant? Do you think Blacks and other minorities are going to be more militant? Women? Don't you understand that defeat demoralizes people? Defeat convinces people that you can't beat city hall. If Ford wins, it will be understood by every political person in the United States and the world as a move to the right and people will act accordingly.

On the other hand, if Carter wins, we are not going to get the New Jerusalem. If Carter wins, he will do some horrendous things—I guarantee it. I don't have to be told it, I know it. But if Carter wins, he will also do some good things. But more than that, the conditions of a Carter victory are the conditions for that, the conditions of a Carter victory are the conditions for working class militancy, and the militancy of minority groups, and the militancy of women, and the militancy of the democratic reform movement. We can actually begin to make victories on full employment, national health, and issues like that.

Those nonvoters out there are not going to be convinced by a brilliant speech. They are not going to be convinced by a marvelous article. They will be convinced when they see a political movement actually deliver. What has turned them off is the feeling that political movements don't deliver. And if we get Ford, they will be turned off. If we get Carter, there is the possibility, an infinitely greater possibility, they can be involved. They can be brought back into politics.

Which is why the Democratic Socialist Organizing Committee, those of us in it, have participated in the Democratic Party. We've gone in with "socialist" very clear on our sweatshirt. We're not "boring from within." We're not conspirators. That's why I testified at the national platform hearing. That's why we were the organizers of the, I think, the best left-wing meeting at the Democratic Party convention.

We do not accept the Democratic Party as it is. We seek to transform it. But we go with the real live workers and minority groups and women where they are. We do not make our conditions to them. We only want to work with them to transform the society.

Last point: next fall when the City of New York begins again the process of destroying City University—and I tell you, it is likely that it will—next fall when the City of New York may well begin the process of destroying Queens College, you will not get any help from President Ford, you will not get any help from President Peter Camejo because he will not be president. If Gerald Ford is president, *you will not get any help*. If Jimmy Carter is president, there is the possibility—which is so much better than the certitude of Gerald Ford spitting in our eye that it is something to vote for.

There is a difference tomorrow. We need every vote we can get in this country. Therefore, I say to you, tomorrow vote for Carter, not with illusions that he is going to change American society radically. He will not. But with the clear understanding that he is the superior alternative on issues of life and death for ordinary people, the majority of the people of the United States.

And with the understanding that—of those of us who are for democratic social and radical and socialist change and are part of the mass movement and not counterposed to it—his victory can be a starting point for the transformation, the debates on the issues, the alternatives which this society doesn't have now but might get through a Carter victory and will be denied through a Ford victory.

Therefore, I say, in that spirit and for those reasons, you should vote for Carter tomorrow.

PETER CAMEJO: There is one error in what Mr. Harrington said about where the Socialist Workers Party stands. What we say is not that the solution is for you to go into the ballot box on November 2 and vote Socialist Workers Party as *the* solution. In fact, we think what happens tomorrow is so much less significant than other things that are happening in this country that part of the problem is the myth that you are making the decision tomorrow about who governs this country or what will happen.

To us, it is the independent mass movements of the people themselves—like the antiwar movement in the streets—that affected American history in a positive way. Like the mass civil rights movement, like the mass labor movement, like the mass women's movement—these are the social forces that have made America move forward and this is the key to our entire strategy. This is why we challenge and disagree with the Democratic Socialist Organizing Committee, whose strategy is to join the Democratic Party, a party which is not known to have called a single antiwar demonstration or a single pro–civil rights demonstration.

Not once has the Democratic Party called out the National Guard to make sure a strike wins, although it controls most cities, states, and—much of the time—the federal government. It has never acted on your behalf and my behalf. It has never acted to advance the rights of women. In fact, what poor Michael has to do is . . . I feel sorry for him. In order to convince you to vote for Carter, he's got to talk about Ford.

Let's look at Carter. Where does Carter stand? He said Carter is against the sale of arms. Carter was for the war in Vietnam from the beginning to the end, for genocide in Vietnam. He's a man who called a state holiday to support [Lt. William] Calley when he was on trial for ordering the execution of two- and three-year-olds. That's where Carter stood on the question of war.

While we were in the streets fighting against the war in Vietnam, when the majority of the American people were against the war in Vietnam, this man was saying we *should* be in Vietnam—fighting for us to stay in Vietnam, and opposing the antiwar movement.

Today Carter is talking about whether or not there's going to be amnesty, and he does it by tricky wording so he leaves out the overwhelming majority of the people—those who refused to violate Article I, Section 8, of the U.S. Constitution, which says we cannot go to war without a declaration of war. Did we declare war? No.

That war was illegal and anyone who refused to fight was not violating American law. Instead of talking about amnesty for them, we should be talking about whether we give Carter and Ford and the people who got us into that war amnesty. That's what we should be talking about.

Talk about the rights of women. Where does Carter stand on the rights of women? He's opposed to women's right to abortion, just like Ford. The majority in this country believe it's a woman's right to choose.

Death penalty: Carter's for the death penalty. He signed

it into law in Georgia. The first person that was going to be executed was going to die on October 26 in Georgia. The majority of people on death row in Georgia are Black. Where does Carter stand? For the death penalty.

We can go down and down and down the list. On the labor movement. Carter's got his own factory. You want to know how he treats labor? No unions allowed in his factory. He pays the minimum wage. He pays white workers more than he pays Black workers. He's for right-to-work laws, that is, nonunion laws. That's what he stands for. He makes it clear. He makes it explicit.

You heard debates for four-and-a-half hours. Did you hear a proposal for how to end unemployment? I'll tell you how we have to end unemployment. We've got to stop wasting $115 billion on war and use the money for jobs. We've got to stop wasting the $60 billion in interest payments that is being given to the rich.

What is the problem in New York City? Why are we having these cutbacks? Michael said that there'll be hope for us if Carter's in office. I mean, it's an insult to our intelligence. Who is running New York City? Which party? His [Harrington's] party. The party he belongs to. The party he urges you to join. The party that he urges you to vote for is running this city.

What is the Democratic Party doing to the people of this city? It is closing our schools. It is closing our hospitals. It has laid off 50,000 workers. Why? Because it wants to pay $2 billion in interest to the richest people of this country. Have you heard a single Democrat get up and say, "Instead of paying $2 billion in interest, we should use this money to put people back to work"?

I want to ask you a question. What would happen if we had a referendum tomorrow in New York City between what Mr. Harrington's party, the Democratic Party, stands for—that we close the schools, close the hospitals, keep 50,000 people laid off, make five- and six-year-olds pay to go to school because they can't have free buses anymore, have the fire department, the sanitation department closed—or the Socialist Workers Party's proposal that we give all these people back their jobs, reopen the schools, reopen the hospitals?

The Democrats say we have to pay the $2 billion to the rich. We say let's not give one tax dollar to anybody who's making over $40,000. No welfare for the rich. It would balance the New York City budget, give us a surplus, and put everybody back to work. Now you tell me whose side the majority would be on in that referendum.

I'll tell you the problem in this country: The problem is, no other point of view is heard except the point of view that sides with the corporations. The problem is that Carter and Ford are both for the rich, both for the corporations, both for this system. They are both for a system that puts profits over human needs. And the problem is, *no other point of view is heard.*

What we are proposing is not that the solution is simply to vote for the Socialist Workers Party. We say we must look at the political arena and the problems that are taking place in the government today in the same way we did in the fight against the war in Vietnam.

We were a tiny minority. Michael Harrington says you have to go with the workers. The majority of the workers in this country were for the war in Vietnam. Does that mean we should have been for it? Sometimes the majority is wrong.

A majority in this country was once for slavery. But the abolitionists went outside the two-party system, didn't they? They ran their own candidates, didn't they? Did they have a chance to win? No. The Harringtons of the 1840s were telling them, "You're messing things up. Do you want the slave owners party to get in, the Democrats? You better vote for the Whigs."

Now when we look back in history, what do we say about

these abolitionists? They were right! They did the right thing because they went out and started preaching to everyone, "No, both parties are wrong. Both parties are for slavery. Even though one says they'll hit the slave with a mild whip and the other one says with a heavy whip." The abolitionists said, "That's not the real issue. The problem is, we've got to build a movement, we've got to build a new mass party that'll fight slavery."

And which way would you have voted in 1840, Harrington? Would you have voted for the abolitionists or for the two parties, for the "liberal" party of the slave owners, for the Whigs?

I say today we've got to break with the whole concept that we have to vote for the lesser evil; that is, we have to vote for evil, that we have to go out and support candidates that are against our interests—why? Because they put up somebody else that's worse.

The people that run this country can *always* find somebody else that's worse. They want you to stomach Carter, they put up Ford. If they want you to vote for Mussolini, they'll run Hitler. They'll use every argument you've heard today to explain why we shouldn't vote for Hitler, we should vote for Mussolini. "Well, are you going to tell me there's no difference?"

Let's have no illusions. Whether you vote for Carter or Ford, you are not making any decision about who runs this government. That is a myth. We must fight that myth.

The corporations run this country. The oil industry gets the secretary of state no matter who wins, Democrat or Republican, every time. The undersecretaries and the cabinet posts, the people who really write the laws, are the people who will continue to run the country no matter who gets elected. Both these parties represent the same class. The rich have two parties. We have none. That's the problem. That's what we must go out and tell people.

We must go out and tell people the truth about the Democratic Party. It's a war party; it's a racist party; it's a sexist party; and it's antilabor. And the minute you start telling people to join such a party, you've undermined your entire ability to have a strategy for social change.

And that's why the Democratic Socialist Organizing Committee and Michael Harrington—who is personally absolutely dedicated to having a better society, and certainly opposed to the massacre that took place in Vietnam—found themselves stuck in their strategy during the entire antiwar movement. They were unable to become really heavy participants—as I'm sure, looking back now, they wish they had been—because their strategy of being members of the party that was carrying out the war made it sort of hard to explain to people how you should fight the war—by joining the party that conducts the war.

Look, let me give you an example: Carter got up and said he was for "ethnic purity," and then he said he made a slip. He said he was against "Black intrusion," and then said he made a slip. I want to ask you a question. When's the last time you slipped and said "ethnic purity"? When's the last time you heard *anybody* "slip" and say "ethnic purity"?

I'll tell you why you haven't heard anybody use that word. Because after Adolf Hitler died that word *purity* associated with race became very unpopular. It was popularized under the Nazis and it's a term that's not used.

Carter says he made a slip. He made no slip. He makes it clear. He says, "Well, the problem, you know, is America is into this neighborhood thing. Irish like to live around Irish, Italians around Italians, Jews around Jews." You know how it is in America. Italian moves next door to an Irish. They get very upset. There have been several riots recently of Irish. You know, a German moves in across the street from a Swede, several Germans have had their houses burned down because the Swedes don't like it.

Listen, you know and I know exactly what Jimmy Carter was talking about and what Ford was talking about, and they both talk about the exact same thing. They're saying, "Keep Blacks out." All this business about neighborhoods and keeping the ethnicity up of neighborhoods is nothing but cover-up, double-talk for racism and continuing housing discrimination.

And once you get in with these people and you start trying to justify it, you start falling into it. It's very sad to say that Michael Harrington himself has fallen for this.

He writes in his latest book, "If minority demands for quality education through integration were, and should have been, the dominant consideration, still, ethnic and class concerns for the integrity of neighborhoods. . . ." "Class concerns for the integrity of neighborhoods"? I'll tell you which class has concern over the integrity of their neighborhood. ". . . Class concerns for the integrity of neighborhoods were not simply a mask for racism, they derived from an authentic emotion."

I'd like to ask you in the summary to state what "authentic emotion" are you talking about when Jimmy Carter says that he wants an ethnically pure neighborhood? I'll tell you what that "emotion" is. The word for it is *racism*. That's the word for it.

You pull the lever for the Democrats and Republicans, you're voting for unemployment, inflation, racism, sexism. Talk about unemployment and the Hawkins-Humphrey bill. That's an insult to the intelligence because that bill does not provide a single job. You know what that bill says? It says it shall be the policy of the United States government that there be almost full employment and that the Congress is authorized to pass the necessary legislation to achieve it.

Now, there's one thing that all of the Hawkins-Humphrey bill supporters never mention. It's that the bill was already passed in 1947 under a different name. It's called the Full

Employment Act, which made it the law of the land that the government would have full employment and Congress was authorized to pass all the necessary legislation to make full employment.

So what we're told is: You see, Carter's better because he promises to pass a motion that will promise that we'll have jobs. If the Democrats, Mr. Harrington's party, had a concrete proposal, they could make it. They run the Congress and the Senate. They run the city. They run the state.

Now, how many times will they tell us we've got to vote for them. We've already tried it, haven't we? Michael Harrington was telling me, "Vote for Lyndon Baines Johnson, otherwise we'll end up in a war." And the Socialist Workers Party was saying, "No. As long as the working people have no party of their own, that's when they'll be taking us to war."

We said in the *Militant* before the 1964 elections, regardless of whether Goldwater or Lyndon Baines Johnson gets elected we are going into a war in Vietnam. We said the best thing to do is to register a protest vote against both.

I'll tell you what'll bring social change and the most effective way to use our vote is if millions of people in this country began to refuse to vote Democrat or Republican. That would put more pressure on the government to have to bend to the demands.

He said the Democrats are where the workers go. Where are the workers going? The majority aren't going to vote. That's where the workers are going. They're turning their backs on the Democrats and Republicans.

In the primaries, 80 percent of the American people didn't vote. Carter got 4.2 percent. The working class in this country is over 90 percent. So where do you tell me the workers are going for Carter? Workers in Georgia certainly aren't going for Carter. When he ran for governor there, 93 percent of the Blacks voted against him. Of course, then he was an open racist; now he's an undercover, closet racist.

No, the mass of the people are turning their backs on the Democratic and Republican parties because they see in both these parties no answer to their problems.

So, what should we be doing? Running around like Michael, sincerely, but incorrectly, saying, "Please, please, come back. Please, come back. Look, I know the party has been racist, it's been sexist, it's for the war in Vietnam, and it threw you out of work, and it created enormous unemployment.

"I know it's created inflation, and it's lowered your wages, and women are only making 54 percent of what men make—that's 5 percent worse than it was six years ago—and Blacks are making 56 percent of what whites make, and that's 5 percent worse. I know all this is happening. But please, don't leave us. Come back, come back. . . . What do you want—Ford?"

What we should be saying to people is: You're right in leaving these two parties. But the problem is that that's not the solution. What we need is to build a new party, a party of labor in this country.

That is already beginning. The Raza Unida Party has appeared in the Southwest. It's an independent party of Chicanos. It has won the elections in several cities, like Crystal City in Zavala County, Texas.

I want to ask Mr. Harrington a question here that he must answer: If he were in Zavala County, would he vote for the Raza Unida Party or for his party? Would he vote for the majority party, a party of workers that already exists, or would he vote for the party of the bosses, the Democratic Party in Texas? Which party would he vote for?

We say, vote for the Raza Unida Party to the Texas workers and to Chicanos.

Now, if he's for voting for the Raza Unida Party in Zavala County, why not advocate that Blacks form their own party in Detroit, where they're a majority, and take it over and run it in their interests and the interests of all working people?

Why shouldn't we advocate that working people break with the Democratic Party and form their own party?

I'll tell you the most important election taking place this year, and it's not this election taking place November 2. It's an election in which Mr. Harrington and myself are both on the same side.

I want to say in this debate that we're arguing about a strategic question. There are many, many points of agreement between us. One of the problems we always have on the left is that we seem to talk only about differences. We should spend a lot of time talking about where we have agreement and where we can work together.

One of those points is the most important election taking place in this country, which is Ed Sadlowski's effort to win control of the steelworkers' union for the rank-and-file worker. Here's a rebellion taking place in the largest and most important union of the AFL-CIO, which could put that union back into the hands of working people.

They've already won in the largest district. If they win nationwide and this spreads into other unions, that will create the potential to build a mass labor party in this country that would put human needs before profits. And that is the solution. The building of an independent party of *our class*.

It is not true that the Carter-Ford conflict is a conflict of two classes. It is like a ping-pong game. They have to have two. How long would you watch it if there was only one playing? Then everybody tries to figure out who's worse. The polls show that 48 percent think that Ford is worse and 47 percent think that Carter's worse. And everybody's going in to see if they can stop the other one.

Carter went so far as to knock McCarthy off the ballot in New York so people who wanted to vote for McCarthy couldn't, so Carter can get the votes of people who don't even want to vote for him. Now, is that what you want? Is that the type of society we're talking about?

I think we should have a debate. He says with Carter we can have a debate. We had four-and-a-half hours and we didn't hear any debate. All we heard was the "Great Agreement." No, we're not going to have a debate until we get off our knees and stand up and recognize that the Democratic and Republican parties are not our parties; that working people, Black people, women, Chicanos, Puerto Ricans need to build our own mass party. And, like the early abolitionists, we get up and say it even if we're a tiny minority.

We say we need to put human needs before profits. That's the basic problem. We've got to break with the Democratic Party, put up our own candidates, and tell the full truth to the American people: that the Democratic Party does not represent them. Thank you.

QUESTIONS

QUESTION: One of the top union leaders in New York City, Victor Gotbaum, is a member of the Democratic Socialist Organizing Committee, which is Mr. Harrington's group. According to all the press, the bankers have been very proud to say that Mr. Gotbaum has been the most conciliatory and the most cooperative in agreeing to laying off tens of thousands of workers in his union.

Isn't this the proof of how your strategy leads to a dead end? Victor Gotbaum told the workers and the poor people in New York City in 1973 and 1974 to vote for the liberal, Mayor [Abraham] Beame, and the liberal, Governor [Hugh] Carey, on the basis that they would *not* lay off, that they would *not* cut back, that they would *not* end free tuition. These were the issues that were debated.

Gotbaum said, you can be sure if a Republican gets in

these things will happen, but if Beame and Carey get in, we'll have a chance because they're more sensitive. It seems like now I'm having a *déjà vu* with Ford.

HARRINGTON: The essence of the question is: Vic Gotbaum is a member of DSOC. He told people to vote for the Democrats. The Democrats are in control of New York. Isn't this the dead-end [policy] of DSOC since Gotbaum is losing jobs? OK?

A couple of answers. Number one: If you analyze seriously the New York City crisis, you must know that it is a national crisis caused by the government following corporate priorities, creating massive unemployment created by Republicans. It is solvable in the immediate only in Washington, which is one of the reasons I'm for Carter. Beame can't solve it. Carey can't solve it. They don't have the resources. The only way you can solve it is in Washington, D.C. It's not going to be solved by Gerald Ford—we know what he does to us.

Secondly, two things about Vic Gotbaum. Number one: The DSOC is not a democratic centralist nucleus of the future party of the power of the proletariat. We are a catalyst.

We know that socialism's a joke in America. It is not a serious political movement. It is not. Go out in this country. It is not a serious political movement. Therefore, we don't have the pretenses of being a vanguard party. We don't discipline our members.

Finally, let me say that I think Vic Gotbaum—in a bitter struggle created by corporations and Republicans who are going to vote for Ford—has done a better job under absolutely miserable and intolerable conditions of defending his membership than any trade unionist I know in New York City.

CAMEJO: I want to say very briefly I think the way we should take care of the political crisis we have in New York would be to get Gotbaum and all the other union leaders—including Michael Harrington—together. And for us to put up our own labor slate and to take over the city and run it in the interests of human needs, instead of having these politicians who are obviously running it for the corporations.

Instead, what [Gotbaum and Harrington] do is crawl after Beame and the others. It's perfectly true. Gotbaum and Harrington both said to vote for Beame. You tried it. Did it work? Why don't you try it again? We've done it for a hundred years. It never worked yet. What the hell, give it another hundred years. Maybe someday it'll start working.

I say it's about time that working people, the majority, started putting up our own candidates and putting our own people, that we control democratically, in office. The Democratic Party is the least democratic of any party in this country.

QUESTION: In the newspaper this morning there was a story in reference to a Black minister being turned away from the church in which Jimmy Carter is a deacon in Plains, Georgia. I would like to hear Mr. Camejo's response to the implications of that action for Mr. Carter's attitudes toward Blacks if and when he becomes elected president.

CAMEJO: I don't give this thing that much importance. You see, the fact is that, regardless of what the laws of the land are, Jimmy Carter has supported discrimination and racism in Georgia all along. Now, Mr. Harrington knows this.

When he was on the school board in Georgia after the 1954 Supreme Court decision, Mr. Carter did nothing for integration. All the white children were bused to school. Blacks had to walk. He even made a motion to have a Black school moved so whites wouldn't have to see Blacks on their way to school. So this has been his position. It's true he's not an extreme, extreme racist. He didn't himself personally go out and beat up Blacks. He left that to others.

Today on the real issue of affirmative action for Blacks, he's opposed to it. Busing, which is absolutely necessary, and which Mr. Harrington's for, Carter's against.

Who runs the city of Boston? The Democrats. Who have been the people who have allowed the racists to meet in city hall in Boston? The Democrats. Who has made the city, with taxpayers' money, finance the lawsuit of Boston racists against Blacks? The Democrats. So why don't we join them?

That's Mr. Harrington's solution, because he says Mr. Carter is better. With that argument, you know, you can go anywhere you want. Yes, it's true, Carter has a long history of racism. He himself has to have a myth. Because he can't cover it all up, although he does try to deny some of the more extreme things.

HARRINGTON: A couple of things. Number one: Banning the Black minister from joining the church is intolerable. Number two: Take care—it could be a setup. The SWP knows something about setups. You might think about that. Number three: What would Carter do for the Blacks? Much, much more than Gerald Ford, because he would follow full employment policies that would make it possible for Black people to begin making the gains again that were made—not enough—but gains that were made in the 1960s.

Last point: Peter Camejo throughout . . . I mean, he's got Carter as such a scoundrel—then isn't it surprising that Coretta King and Andy Young, and the Black people of the United States are such dummies that they can't see through an out-and-out closet racist? What a contemptuous attitude this is toward the leadership and the masses of the Black people in the United States who have not seen through such an obvious racist. Doesn't this suggest to you it might be just a bit more complicated than Mr. Camejo presents it?

QUESTION: I'm from the Revolutionary Student Brigade at Queens College. Mr. Harrington slandered Marx. And as long as he did, I'd like to ask him to respond to this quote from Lenin. [Questioner reads a long quotation from Lenin explaining that capitalist states are repressive.]

HARRINGTON: I'm sort of at a loss. The reason I'm at a loss is that I love playing quotationmanship. I am, as any of my students in the audience here will tell you, one of the most dedicated Marx quoters in the world.

I don't know. Lenin said that states are repressive institutions, and that political gains are often shell games. Absolutely agreed. However, I also think that tomorrow there is a significant choice for New York City, for working people, for Black people, for women.

I want to change that state, but I do not think a Vladimir Ilyich Lenin—analyzing politics from the point of view of an underground movement under tsarism and the dictatorship afterwards—is the best philosopher to tell us what to do on November 2, more than fifty years after his death. So I finesse. I pass.

CAMEJO: It is true that Marx, Lenin, and others in the past have always opposed workers voting for parties of the ruling class. Marx made a big speech about it in 1851 which ends with the statement, workers should never vote democrat—that is, small *d*, meaning procapitalist forces—but should always put up their own candidates. But I'm not for getting into the quoting game either.

I'd like to take advantage of this thirty seconds I have left to answer the accusation that I'm insulting Blacks. Black people are not voting for Carter, Mr. Harrington, and you know it and you shouldn't join the lie. The majority, the overwhelming majority of Blacks, in spite of their misleaders who tell them to vote for Carter, aren't voting for Carter.

In the primaries they said Carter was getting the Black vote. Down in Miami the first time, they announced this during the primaries. Do you know what percentage of Blacks voted? Four. Carter got two. So they said the Blacks are voting for Carter. You know how many Blacks voted in Bedford-Stuyvesant for Carter? Less than 5 percent. The majority of the Blacks agree with me that neither of them are any good, and that's what Black people are voting this year. Let's tell the truth.

I don't care what any Black leaders say. I know where Andrew Young is going. A man who would get up on television before this nation and say there's no more racism in Georgia. And then say it's because of Jimmy Carter. I almost fell off my chair. I thought it was "Mission Impossible."

QUESTION: I'd like to direct this to Mr. Camejo. I for one—and I know many other people—am going to walk into that voting booth tomorrow and stare at that first line. And I'm going to say, "Do I vote for the short term or do I vote for the long term?" And my choice is truly between Camejo and Carter.

What can I say to myself in January when I vote for Camejo and I go up to Albany to lobby for City University, and they're telling me that there's no money, that Beame has said that he's not going to fund us? What can I say to myself when I have nowhere else to turn when I vote for you and Gerald Ford is in Washington? How do I reconcile the fact that I'm going to have nowhere to turn anymore—aside from a long-term perspective—when I want to graduate next year and my university isn't going to be there when the doors open in February?

CAMEJO: You're saying the same thing that young people asked me in 1964 when they said, "I'd like to vote Socialist Workers, but I've got to vote Lyndon Baines Johnson or we'll be in a war in Vietnam. What am I going to say if I vote socialist and then we all get drafted and I have to go to Vietnam to kill Vietnamese? How am I going to justify it to myself?"

You're going to go to Albany and it's going to be Carter that's going to be cutting you back. And you're going to be coming up to me and saying, "Mr. Camejo, you were right." I'm ready to bet on that. I'll tell you what: the day we turn around and give a half a million, a million votes to an independent socialist candidate, you will suddenly see a change in this country. Because the message we've got to send with a socialist vote is—not to Washington, but to the tens of millions of people who are turned off—"Brothers and sisters, you're not alone."

The time has come for us to start standing up. That is the best way for us to win reforms. You want to save this school? Then don't give a vote to the Democrats and Republicans. That's not going to make them bend to your pressure. You want the demonstrations to work? Then you've got to have the growing political power of an independent force behind them. Because as long as they've got the political monopoly, you demonstrate all you want and they keep smiling at you.

Then they'll put up two candidates. They'll always have one that's worse than the other—just mathematically, unless they're exactly equal. Then you'll come and give the same speech to me ten years from now and twenty years from now.

We'll have wars and we'll have inflation, we'll have pollution—everything—until we stand up and start doing it. That's what's going to stop them. It doesn't matter whether Carter or Ford gets in. That's irrelevant for what the corporations are going to do. When the ruling class wanted Lyndon Baines Johnson to bomb, he bombed. When they wanted him not to bomb, he didn't bomb. It would have been the same, regardless.

This idea that when you vote tomorrow, you're deciding who runs this government, is a myth. You still believe it? Go ahead and vote for Carter. Then come and let's have a talk in January. It won't be January, it has to be February. But we'll have a talk and you'll see.

HARRINGTON: Quick quotationmanship. Marx supported at least two bourgeois candidates that I can think of. One named Abraham Lincoln, the other named Andrew Johnson. Leave that aside.

Camejo is wrong. There will be a difference when you go to Albany if Ford is in or if Carter is in. Anybody who is political in this audience knows it. I can't prove that—that is so ABC. Everybody knows it.

Secondly, and more important, I think the way to send a message to the people turned off—you can't send them a card, you can't go and give a speech on television—would be if we could turn City University around just a bit on open admissions and free tuition. If we could start going back, if we could show them that there's some hope.

What I'm saying is, I repeat, not that Carter's going to do what he should do, or that he'll do enough. I have no illusions about that. He'll be better when you go to Albany.

The way to convince those people is not to give a speech, not to vote SWP, but to show them that CUNY [City University of New York] can be saved as a decent, viable form of higher education for working people, and minorities, and middle class people in New York City.

QUESTION: You keep saying that there is a difference between Ford and Carter and, frankly, I have a hard time seeing it. But I don't think I'm alone on this and it's not just Mr. Camejo. The *Wall Street Journal* in its October 25 editorial says quite frankly that after the election when people go to Washington to ask for more New York City aid, the response will be no different whether Ford or Carter is elected.

I have to agree with them. There are Democrats in now: Beame and Carey. It's not just that they don't have the power to help New York City. They have been the conscious cutting edge in ending this university. They're not some victims of something. They consciously played the role of trying to figure out how best to cut this university.

HARRINGTON: OK. The *Wall Street Journal* has some second thoughts on your editorial. You can find them in today's issue. The *Wall Street Journal* said this morning that the problem with Carter is that he's become too liberal. That's why he's losing. He's going for this full employment stuff. He's not being a conservative; that's why he went down. They say he's moved to the left; that's what's wrong with him.

The *Wall Street Journal* knows what side of the bread the butter is on. Peter Camejo says [the Hawkins-Humphrey bill is] just a sheet of paper. I'm going to get to that in the summary. That's preposterous. The *Wall Street Journal* and all the business people who have been working night and day against Hawkins-Humphrey know that it is not just a sheet of paper. They are afraid. They are afraid that we'll get something out of it.

Last point: The Democratic Party has got to explain to radicals in the audience who belong to Leninist organizations—it might come as a shock—that it is not a Leninist organization. In a Leninist organization, if Camejo says something, you can be sure that the entire Political Committee of the Socialist Workers Party believes it.

I don't like Abe Beame. I don't like all kinds of Democrats. The Democratic Party is filled with charlatans and frauds and antilabor people. I said that. Of course it is. It's also filled with the most progressive forces in America. Is it a contradictory party? Yes. Is this a bourgeois party, the likes of which Karl Marx never dreamed of? Yes. Is this an unprecedented situation? Yes. What do you have to do? Think.

If you think, you'll understand that in this party there are reactionary forces, progressive forces, including the entire progressive wing of the labor movement. I go not with the Democratic Party. It is not my party in a Leninist sense. I go with the left-liberal, labor, trade union, Black, minority, women's wing of the Democratic Party.

CAMEJO: On the question of this difference. There is a difference between the Socialist Workers Party and the

Democratic Party. He says there's a lot of good people in the Democratic Party. That's the truth. But the question is, who runs the party?

In the Socialist Workers Party, the ranks run the party. Harrington may not agree with that. We have rules that when a majority votes to stop at the stop sign, even the minority stops at the stop sign. You know, that's what we do in society as a whole. This sounds very dangerous to Mr. Harrington. I don't know how else you can organize things other than by majority vote—democracy.

Except the way they do it in the Democratic Party. I guess that's why he's against that concept, because in his party they don't do it that way. They can have a majority of workers in it, but the party's run for the rich. We've got to understand who runs the Democratic Party. This Democratic Party and Mr. Carter are not representing working people.

What about this business that they're for full employment? The Democrats run Congress. They run the Senate. Just name what they have proposed for full employment. You say that business is afraid of the Hawkins-Humphrey bill. The ruling class always prefers for us to vote for the most conservative alternative they have. But they always make sure to have another one in case we don't.

Do you think the ruling class is so stupid that they would only put up one candidate and say, "There it is! You want him? Aw, you didn't like him." They're intelligent enough to run two so that you spend your time trying to figure out which one of their [candidates to pick]. They add up the Democratic and Republican vote to figure out what they got. They can have a little debate among themselves as to who they would prefer us to vote for as the best alternative for them. But *both* are their alternatives.

And although Carter may use more demagogy, let me tell you something. The Democratic Party, when it was founded in this country, was the party of the slavocracy. And who belonged to it? The workers and the small farmers—just like they do today. It was the slavocracy that presented bills, like the Hawkins-Humphrey bill—little tokens, gestures to try to win over the workers to be in their party. But the party was run by the slave owners, and today it's run by the people who really run this society.

QUESTION: You say there's no difference between Ford and Carter, but that's just a myth. You believe if Ford gets elected and things get bad, people will say there's no more hope and will go to the socialist party. But the Democratic Party is the only way we can have any hope left for this country.
When you say that Lyndon Baines Johnson did nothing for this country but the Vietnam War, that's utterly absurd. Lyndon Baines Johnson did a lot of good for the economy. And even on Vietnam, Johnson had bad advisers, and he had the honor to resign when he knew his policy was wrong.

CAMEJO: I can't believe this question. Lyndon Baines Johnson said he wouldn't run anymore because there was no chance of his getting elected. Everyone hated him so much. You forget that the man couldn't go anywhere in this country without tens of thousands coming out and yelling, "Hey, hey, LBJ, how many kids did you kill today?" Don't tell me he wasn't for the war in Vietnam, somebody put him in it. Let's deal with reality. Let's not deal with these myths they make.

You say that we're voting for the worse. No, you're just falling for their trap. The FBI—right now they have sixty-six agents in my campaign committee to try to destroy it. I wrote Carter and asked him to make a statement against that. He won't. Because he's for that. He's for that. Just like the red squad in Atlanta under his control was for going after the Black movement and the socialist movement to destroy them. They'll continue to do that. Because you've got to understand what the problem is.

The problem is we haven't built our own alternative.

What you say to the people here is, "Don't start your own alternative. Don't start voting socialist. Don't promote the break from the Democratic and Republican parties and start building our own thing. Because, you see, if you do that, Ford will get in."

That argument will keep us always in chains. We'll never have our own party. We'll never have an alternative. We'll always be having to pick one of theirs, if we accept your premise. I say, let's be very daring and challenge. Let's have real democracy in this country. Why should it be that if you vote socialist, it's really a vote for Ford?

Look at how they took Eugene McCarthy off the ballot. Why can't we have democratic laws in this country so there's proportional representation? If 10 percent wanted McCarthy, then that point of view gets 10 percent of the seats. If 5 percent want the socialists, they get that percent of the seats, so that every vote counts.

They could pass that tomorrow. They don't want democracy in this country. They want to play a trick on you. They want the electoral laws to be so geared that you don't have a choice. In California, with 65 signatures the Democrats get put on the ballot. Socialists have to get 99,284. They make the financing law so only they get finances. Socialist candidates or anybody else that's in opposition can't get financing.

We have two government parties that perpetuate themselves. And you fall for their argument of thinking you always have to vote for the people governing the United States—and that you cannot vote for opposition. They've written the law to make it that way so that oppositions will not appear. It's about time we don't get fooled by these electoral laws and recognize we don't have real democracy in this country.

People who want to vote for Eugene McCarthy are not voting for him because of this logic. People should be free to vote for whatever position they want. And every vote should count, and that could be done very easily through election laws. The Democrats and Republicans won't do it. And Mr. Harrington falls for that and never speaks out against it in this type of debate.

HARRINGTON: Number one: Lyndon Johnson was tragically wrong on the subject of Vietnam. He went into it for a pile of reasons. He wasn't just tricked into it. And he was stopped, not just by the antiwar movement in the streets, which did some excellent things, but by the political struggle in the Democratic Party of Gene McCarthy and Bobby Kennedy. We took it into the Democratic Party. When Johnson was challenged in the Democratic Party and he was going to be defeated by McCarthy and Kennedy, that's when he backed out.

Secondly, you're right, there was a difference even during this horrible war in Vietnam. Goldwater would not have given us Medicare. Tell me there's no difference about Medicare.

Thirdly, there is a theory which I call the "vulture theory" of socialism. It says the worse things get, the more radical people will get. Nonsense. What makes people radical is the feeling that they can win something. What's going to make people conservatives tomorrow is if Ford wins. What will open the way to a possible radicalization is if Carter wins.

QUESTION: Mr. Harrington, how can you tell women to vote for Carter? Neither he nor his party has been fighting for women's rights.

HARRINGTON: Look, you tell me your Jimmy Carter horror story and I'll tell you mine. I'm not saying he didn't do many things I'm against. He's not my candidate. I am saying this: He is the better candidate for women.

Number one: His position on abortion is not the same as Ford's. Ford is for a constitutional amendment. Carter is not.

Number two: I was at the Democratic convention where the politically organized women of the United States were there in massive presence. They were a tremendous, effective pressure inside the Democratic Party at that convention on Carter about women's representation. They got concessions out of him.

Number three: Carter will appoint people to the Supreme Court who will not be like the Neanderthals that Gerald Ford is going to give you on the Supreme Court on issues like abortion.

And four: I would suggest to you that, in addition to the Equal Rights [Amendment], which I am committed to, which the main progressive forces inside the Democratic Party—the trade union movement, the Coalition of Labor Union Women, the Congressional Black Caucus—are all committed to, the most important single thing that can be done for women in the United States, is to gain full employment in this country. Because as long as we don't have full employment, men are pitted against women, Blacks and other minorities against whites, organized against unorganized.

I'm saying, on all these issues—abortion, the way the courts will handle women, the whole political atmosphere in the United States, above all the full employment making real affirmative action possible—the choice is between Carter and Ford, and Carter is much, much better for women.

CAMEJO: First, I notice how Michael is more and more turning something into fact by repeating it. And that's that Carter's for full employment. Carter in the debates openly said that his goal after four years is to only have 4.5 percent unemployment. So, he himself advocated 4 million people being unemployed in the debate.

He doesn't even claim to be for full employment, and the fact is that he won't even get to the 4.5 percent because the forces that create unemployment and inflation are totally out of the hands of the president of the United States. They defend a profit-oriented system.

Whether Carter's in or Ford's in, they're both going to have it. And we should have this debate automatically rescheduled for six months from now if Carter wins. I think Mr. Harrington will have much more doubt about having the debate then.

I just want to mention something real quick on the Supreme Court. What did Carter say during the debates? He said he likes the present Nixon Supreme Court. That's what Carter said. What can I do? I can't help you. I'm sorry. You say it's a terrible Supreme Court, it's getting worse. You're right. But he likes it. So, I don't understand what your point is.

QUESTION: I'd like to know Mr. Camejo's position on the question, "the worse, the better."

CAMEJO: Yes. I want to say that I agree with Mr. Harrington. I think that defeats only set people back. It's victories that inspire people—like when masses of women came out and fought for the right to abortion or when we had mass demonstrations against the war in Vietnam and were able to force American troops out of Vietnam. By the way, the two forces that did this were the antiwar movement and the Vietnamese, not the antiwar movement and a bunch of Democrats. Those were the two forces that did it.

But where I differ with Mr. Harrington is not on this. I don't think it's fair to say that that's our position. I think that Michael knows that's not the Socialist Workers Party's position. We do not believe the worse, the better. On the contrary, we believe it's only on the basis of victories that you move forward. I agree with him.

What we're debating is, which is the victory? That's what we're debating. Honestly and sincerely, I believe completely that Mr. Harrington's purpose in wanting Carter is to get full employment, is to get the type of things that we're both for.

I accept his complete sincerity. I say it's more of a victory if half a million people go out and vote socialist than if Carter gets in. I think that's more of a victory. I say that that'll inspire people, rather than once again, twiddle-dee—Oh, I'm sorry. Usually it's twiddle-dee-dee and twiddle-dee-dum. This year we've got two twiddle-dee-dums. I don't think that makes a difference.

HARRINGTON: Half a million people vote socialist, let's take that generous estimate, OK—put that there. Gerald Ford is elected president of the United States. Everybody feels the country is going to the right, unemployment gets deeper, the Supreme Court gets more reactionary because a Democratic Party institutionally in terms of the class and social forces it represents is a more liberal party than a conservative party.

We have four years of reactionary leadership in Washington in which national health gets vetoed; in which we lose on ERA; in which we lose on Hawkins-Humphrey. I don't think that the Socialist Workers Party has the theory that the worse is the better. I think it has the practice that leads to the reality that the worse is the better.

QUESTION: I came into the socialist movement in the 1930s when we were faced with a choice between Roosevelt and the reactionary Republican Party. We got Roosevelt and he took money from relief and for other human things and put it into the war budget. Then we went into war. Under Roosevelt they put eighteen members of the Socialist Workers Party in jail for opposing the war. Then we got the witch-hunt under Truman, another Democrat.

Aren't you proposing the same policy that the Communist Party preached at that time—a policy of supporting the Democratic Party as the "labor coalition," as the "people's party"? Now you want us to take that same road. No, I say we've got to have a *class-struggle* policy.

Your policy is the same as the Mensheviks used in Russia. But Lenin said, we've got to build an independent class party, a Leninist party.

HARRINGTON: Let me defend American Menshevism with just one brief comment. Franklin Roosevelt saved capitalism. I'm a socialist. I'm not terribly enthusiastic about that. However, I do think Franklin Roosevelt should not be accused of having invented World War II.

There was a movement called the Nazi movement. There was a movement called Japanese imperialism, and they had something to do with it. Although I was a conscientious objector during the Korean War, and struggled against the war in Vietnam, I happen to think that World War II was a just, moral, and good war. I'm not against World War II. Now if people think it was an imperialist war, that there was no difference between us and the Nazis, OK.

Second, my policy is very much like the Communist policy in the 1930s. You bet your life it is. I'm an opponent of communist dictatorship and totalitarianism. But while the Socialist Party and the Socialist Workers Party were getting absolutely nowhere because they counterposed themselves to the workers who wanted to vote for Roosevelt, the Communist Party of the 1930s was building the biggest, largest movement calling itself socialist in the United States since the days of Gene Debs, and winning leadership in a third of the unions of the CIO.

At that time the Socialist Party was driving Walter Reuther out because, on the basis of the class struggle in Michigan, he wanted to support Frank Murphy for governor. When the Socialist Party, which I belonged to for many years, did something that idiotic we were counterposing ourselves to the actual political movement of the workers.

There are many things wrong with the Communists, not the least of which is they're agents of Russia politically. But their policy worked.

Now, finally, I'm not in Russia. I'm not a Menshevik. I'm not dealing with Bolsheviks. I'm dealing with America *circa* 1976. In this country, the workers of this country—maybe they're wrong in some aspects of this—see the future of their class in this election, as I've emphasized, with the Democratic Party and Jimmy Carter. I'm with the workers. The Socialist Workers Party is counterposing itself to the workers in the name of the workers. I find that foolish.

CAMEJO: First of all, I'd like to say on the question of what you can blame Roosevelt for and what you can't blame him for. It is true that there was a war, and in this war there was this terrible danger of fascism.

The Socialist Workers Party opposed fascism. We were completely for fighting fascism. All we did was point out the United States government was not really fighting fascism. Otherwise, when they liberated Europe from the fascists, they obviously would have liberated Spain. Instead, they financed fascism in Spain. So, obviously, they had another goal in mind, which was their markets.

When they put the Japanese-Americans into concentration camps, a little thing Roosevelt did in this country, the Socialist Workers Party opposed it. When they bombed Nagasaki and Hiroshima, we stood up alone. We said that was wrong and we opposed it. We went to jail for our opposition to those things. We stood up for our ideals. We said, "The Japanese are just as much human as us and they cannot be blamed for what their government's doing." Our war was not against the Japanese people or against the German people. This government was not fighting for the American people, the Germans, or the Japanese. It was fighting for American corporate interests. That's a simple fact.

Now, as far as the Democratic Party Supreme Court, I just want to say one thing. It's the Democratic Party Supreme Court that denied for seventy years the right of Blacks to vote, the Fifteenth Amendment. So, don't come telling me about the Democratic Party Supreme Court. I could run down a long list of what the Supreme Court has done, whether it's Democrats or Republicans. It's a game. They're the same.

QUESTION: What is the Socialist Workers Party's platform on the Middle East?
CAMEJO: During the Second World War the Jewish people in Europe suffered an enormous holocaust of attempted genocide by German imperialism. During that war the Nazis offered to let 400,000 Jewish people go—actually up to a million in Hungary. The United States refused them.

After the war ended Jewish refugees wanted to come to the United States. The United States refused to let them in. Harrington's party was running the government. Our party established a committee to try and help them to get in. Instead, the Democrats and all the anti-Semites in the world said, "Well, the Nazis weren't able to kill all the Jews, but we've got a new plan. Let's force them into the Middle East to be a beachhead for European and American imperialist interests."

What's happening today in Israel is that the Zionist state (by the way, I'm against theocratic states—states that represent a religion) is oppressing the Palestinian people. I don't think you can justify the oppression of another people because you were once oppressed.

That doesn't mean there isn't anti-Semitism. Right now the army of the United States is run by an anti-Semite. We've got Nixon—did you hear the tapes? Nixon was all for Israel. General Ky, who said we need seven Hitlers in South Vietnam, liked Israel too.

I think the question is quite complex, and what I favor is a democratic, secular Palestine in which both Jews and Muslims can live together with both religious points of view represented. But I favor a state that does not belong to any single religious point of view, and I have the same criticism of Arab states that do the same thing.

HARRINGTON: Let me take up just one point. I believe that Jews and Palestinians both have the right to national self-determination. I believe that Israel is the expression of the Jewish people's right to their self-determination. I support Israel. But I support the right of Palestinians to a state of their own.

The problem is that it has to be negotiated, and you cannot adopt the slogan of a secular, democratic Palestine because that slogan as used by the PLO [Palestine Liberation Organization] has been a cover for "All Jews not here before 1960, get out. All Jews who are Zionists, get out." Whatever the sincerity of people who might hold it, it is a cover for a policy of driving the Jews into the sea. I am for defending the right of Israel and the rights of the Palestinians, but in the Yom Kippur war, the Democratic Socialist Organizing Committee voted in favor of the American government sending whatever military aid was necessary for Israel to defend itself, and I stand by that position.

SUMMARIES

CAMEJO: Let me just take first one minute out of my five-minute summary to say that if the United States were really concerned over the protection of the Jewish people's rights we could have had Israel in this country. We've got a country that's enormous, an entire continent five times the size of Europe. Why didn't we give them part of Virginia—give them all the bombs and planes and everything they want?

The United States doesn't care about the Jewish people. The Democratic and Republican parties and the corporations that run them are anti-Semitic. Don't have illusions about that. Obviously, we can't debate the Middle East here. And I'm sure that Mr. Harrington's position is well intentioned, as I've stated all along. I think that's very important.

But the essence of this debate—the question that just kept getting repeated over and over and over again—is basically this: Is the Democratic Party an institution through which working people, women, Blacks, and Chicanos can make gains; or is it an institution that is run in the interests of the ruling class? That is the real basic debate we've had here.

I say all American history proves beyond a question of a doubt that the Democratic and Republican parties have been run by the same basic interests since 1876. Today the Democratic Party is an institution run for the interests of the corporations and the rich in this country. The promises and the concessions they give us are not because they're in favor of them, it's only insofar as we put mass pressure on them. It is true, if we have mass demonstrations like we did in the antiwar movement, they have to bend towards us because they have to make a decision. It's bad enough they have to lose Vietnam. But they don't want to lose this country, too.

But don't tell me the Democratic Party cares one bit about the people of Vietnam. Let's not rewrite history. When the first referendums were held in this country on the war in Vietnam, Eugene McCarthy urged people to vote for the war. They used his name in the ads. He voted for the Gulf of Tonkin resolution. He voted for all the war appropriations. Eugene McCarthy was for the war in Vietnam. Just like Robert Kennedy was for it.

I debated Ted Kennedy when I ran against him in 1970. I said to him, "Mr. Kennedy, why is it you said you were against the war, but every time it comes up in Congress, you vote for it? You vote for special appropriations. You vote for chemical warfare in Vietnam." He said, "Well, our troops are there. We have to protect them."

Listen, I'm sick and tired of this double-talk. That's all we get from these politicians. They told us they were for stopping the war, but they couldn't do anything about it. When they wanted $200 billion for the war in Vietnam, they had the money. When we asked for education, they said there's no money. This year we're having the largest gross national product ever, one trillion seven hundred billion dollars. Corporate profits are the highest ever, $150 billion.

Mr. Harrington's party controls the Congress, the Senate, the city, and the state. You know what would happen if our party controlled the Congress, the Senate, the city, and the state? But we will never have the working people run the city, the state, or the federal government if we continue to follow his policies, because his policy is for us to join *their* party.

I say break with them. Let the workers have an independent movement. I say: I'm a socialist. I vote socialist. I belong to a socialist party. And, therefore, I call myself a socialist.

I think Mr. Harrington, who's a Democrat, who votes Democrat, supports the Democratic Party, should call himself what he is: a Democrat. And that means to defend capitalism. I know he doesn't want to do that. I know that in his ideology he would like to see socialism. We will never get socialism by supporting capitalism. You will never win equal rights for women by supporting sexists. You will never win the end of racism by supporting racists—even if there are worse racists and worse sexists.

We mustn't fall into the trap of the ballot box myth: You pull the curtain, no one can see what you're doing, then you vote for one of them or you vote for another of them. Then they announce they won again, and you think you decided something.

That is a myth. The decisions are made by much broader social forces, and the key to it is that the workers' movement must be independent. We must favor that the unions break from the Democratic and Republican parties and form their own party. That's what Mr. Harrington won't do. And

I wish he would. I wish we could join together on that, as we have on other things.

I want to just end by thanking Mr. Harrington for this opportunity to debate. I think we need these types of discussions. It's not so much that people are convinced one way or another but we begin to think through the problems of what our strategy should be and how to get change. I know that in the long run, with the impact of events, maybe we'll come closer in our positions in the future and we'll both be together in a labor party. Because when one is formed, even though he's against it, I think he'll join it. Thank you.

HARRINGTON: First, on the sincerity question, I completely agree that what we're debating's bona fide.

Secondly, if masses of American workers got in motion toward the labor party, I would be with them, just as I am now when they're in motion trying to elect Jimmy Carter. That's my key. Where are the politically conscious and organized workers going?

A couple of points. Number one: Peter Camejo's America is an America in which you've got closet racists and out-and-out shills and pimps for the corporations deceiving the Blacks, the working people, et cetera. It is an America in which the Blacks and the workers are pretty dumb. Because if it's as simple, as obvious, as Camejo says, why do all these Black people and working people persist in this error? If one is a Marxist, do you say they're simply befuddled? Or could it be that they might perceive a class interest there, since it is an error they have persisted in now for a generation? I say it's that.

Second: Camejo gives us choices like, you say to the people of New York: We won't pay the interest on the debt, we'll take the $2 billion, we'll restore all the services. What would they do? They'd say, "Hooray!" There's only one problem with that—of course, they'd vote for it. The problem is it's impossible. It is a slogan for socialism in one city. And Camejo, who comes from a movement that knows about socialism in one country, should know it. You don't abrogate your debt to the United States and say, bye-bye. You're part of a nation, you're part of a capitalist system.

I am for taking the profits away from the profiteers—absolutely. That requires a socialist transformation. And I will tell you something, friends: socialism is not going to come soon enough to settle our problems with CUNY [City University of New York] next fall, believe me.

Camejo says, if we could have a socialist solution in New York, wouldn't it be better? Of course it would be better. How do we get to the political possibility of that solution? By counterposing ourselves to workers and other progressive elements who are fighting for Carter and [in that way] helping to elect Ford? Not at all.

Third point: My party, the Democratic Party. Peter Camejo has got a Leninist concept of the Democratic Party. The Democratic Party is a mish-mosh, everybody knows it. I belong to the liberal, trade union, antiwar, Black, feminist, reformist wing of the Democratic Party, where I wear "socialism" on my sweatshirt in very red letters. When I was elected a delegate to the Democratic convention in 1974 from the seventeenth congressional district of New York, I ran publicly as a socialist.

We have held socialist meetings at Democratic Party conventions. When I testified before the Democratic platform committee, I testified as a socialist and I was talking to real working people, and feminists, and other progressive elements. I think that is the way—inside of their party in solidarity and fraternity with them—to then bring up these ideas as part of the common struggle.

Last point: Again, I'm not talking about sincerity, truly I am not. My last point is this: I am for the lesser evil. But Peter Camejo sincerely, decently, unwittingly is for the greater evil because insofar as you vote for him and don't vote for Carter, you are electing Ford.

In Ohio, an SWP candidate getting 100,000 ballots on an independent line two years ago defeated John Gilligan and elected Governor Rhodes, the man who presided over [the 1970 killings at] Kent State. That's the kind of thing you get in America if you play protest politics.

In New York State tomorrow and in the United States as a whole, we need every single vote if we are to get the possibility for this university, this city, this nation to survive. Then, on the basis of a small victory, we need to build a movement which will transform the society and give it, not small victories, but the radical transformation it needs. Thank you.

What is the
Democratic Party coalition?

Jack Barnes vs. Stanley Aronowitz

This debate was part of a conference on political action held at Central Plaza in New York City on October 30, 1965, a few days before the city mayoralty election. The struggle against the Vietnam War was just becoming a mass movement, while the civil rights movement remained an important component of the American political scene. The 1964 presidential election had been the most recent conflict between supporters of independent political action and of the then prevailing Democratic-labor coalition.

Lyndon B. Johnson had been elected president in 1964 with the support of almost all radicals and socialists—the Communist Party, the *National Guardian* newspaper, Social Democrats such as Bayard Rustin and Norman Thomas, and pacifists such as David McReynolds. Students for a Democratic Society had raised the slogan, "Part of the Way With LBJ!" The Socialist Workers Party had run Clifton DeBerry against both Johnson and Goldwater.

Almost every civil rights leader or organization had supported Johnson for president and had agreed to a moratorium on direct actions for civil rights during the election period. The Mississippi Freedom Democratic Party attempted to unseat the regular delegation at the Democratic Party convention in Atlantic City, New Jersey, in August 1964. A compromise, offering the MFDP two seats as at-large delegates, was rejected by the MFDP; the regular delegation walked out of the convention to protest the compromise.

Soon after the election, Johnson began escalating American troop involvement in Vietnam. By the time of this debate, there were about 150,000 American troops in Vietnam. The new antiwar movement had been inaugurated with an SDS-sponsored march on Washington, which drew 20,000 people on April 17, 1965. Between 70,000 and 100,000 people took part in further antiwar actions across the country on October 16, and on November 27, 35,000 demonstrators took part in a march in Washington called by the Committee for a Sane Nuclear Policy (SANE).

The short-lived Committee for Independent Political Action, of which Stanley Aronowitz was a leader, ran James Weinstein on an independent ticket for U.S. representative from New York's nineteenth congressional district in 1966.

This is the first publication of the text of this debate.

What is the Democratic Party coalition?

PRESENTATIONS

JACK BARNES: To understand the present debate over coalitionism, it is necessary to go back to last year's presidential election, when the labor and peace organizations warned that Goldwater would undoubtedly begin systematically bombing North Vietnam and would eventually involve a couple hundred thousand U.S. troops in Vietnam. Thus the necessity of voting for Johnson, supporting the coalition in the Democratic Party. Actually, the high point of this orgy of coalitionism, and what has to be called comic relief, appeared in the *Worker*. The week before the elections, the Communist Party, in an article in the *Worker*, went so far as to chastise the *National Guardian* for having referred to Johnson in an editorial as a lesser evil instead of a positive good. That was the word that was used.

Johnson's landslide victory, with large Democratic majorities in both houses, was portrayed as a victory for peace and progress and for coalitionism. That is, for supporting a candidate that you consider to be an evil, but a lesser evil, and in so doing by some means or other pressuring the Democratic Party in order to mold it to act in the interests of the Negroes, the workers, and the antiwar activists in this country.

Two things, however, blew this idyllic victory for coalitionism apart. The first was the actions of Johnson himself in immediately escalating the vicious war against the Vietnamese. This was met, as most of you remember, with the march in Washington [on April 17, 1965], the first big action of what was to become known as the new student antiwar movement. The march was aimed right against Johnson. I might add that quite a few of those who marched did so with even more determination because they had gone for the lesser evil just a few months before. In fact, one of the most famous signs on the march was carried by a person who obviously was chastising himself; it said, "My lesser evil struck again."

The second thing that tended to blow this whole image of the great coalition apart was the actions and comments of some of the leading coalitionists. Some of the coalitionists who pushed for support for the Texas rancher didn't simply slink away to think the thing over after the effect of their actions became apparent. A group of the most prominent, among them Norman Thomas and Bayard Rustin, signed a statement on the eve of the march on Washington that attempted to red-bait the march, in essence to undermine it and sabotage it.

This was too much. It was bad enough that the man and the party that so many were told to support, and did support, as the peace alternative was calmly carrying out the bloody policy that had been decided months before the election. It was bad enough that this policy had been presented as the private monopoly of the "Defoliator from Arizona." But when those who urged support to LBJ, to avoid escalation, attacked the marchers who protested and opposed Johnson when he did just this—escalated the war—this raised questions, not only about Johnson, not only about the error of supporting him, but about the whole political strategy that would lead these people not only to support him but then to attack those who protested when Johnson carried out what was supposed to be Goldwater's policy. Not only was there something rotten about Johnson's Vietnam policy, there was something basically rotten with the theory of politics that urged you to vote for him and the Democratic Party to avoid this policy, and then became even more vehement in defense of itself when just the opposite occurred.

It was under these conditions that the big debate over coalitionism began in the antiwar movement. Now this debate was, and is mainly, oral, that is, bull sessions and off-the-cuff discussions among the thousands of participants about how best to act politically, and what was the meaning of these various acts. But it has also had a written history. It has included many silent defections from the Democratic Party and some demonstrative acts by people like W. H. Ferry [vice-president of the Fund for the Republic], who openly resigned from the Democratic Party and in essence renounced their whole past political strategy.

Probably the most well-known—I don't say it's the best—single article written attacking coalitionism following this string of events was an article by Staughton Lynd, a young professor from Yale, which appeared in the June–July [1965] issue of *Liberation* magazine. It was basically a rejection of coalitionism and an attack on Rustin. Lynd pointed out that he had discovered, in rethinking the entire question after Rustin's acts around the march on Washington, that this wasn't the first time that Rustin's theory of coalitionism led him to a practice of what, in essence, was counterrevolution. One of the objections to this article was Lynd's strong language, but most of the objections came from those who were sensitive because of their own coalitionist policies.

Lynd said this: "By exaggerating the Johnson coalition's capacity to solve fundamental social problems, and by underestimating the need for independent action by Negroes," Rustin arrived at a stance which leads to nothing but the dissolution of the old civil rights movement and assures that any new movements will not develop in a more radical fashion. He went on further and said: "In opposing the march on Washington against the war in Vietnam Bayard Rustin," who is probably the main public figure among the coalitionists, "has permitted himself to drift into that posture which once evoked epithets such as 'labor lieutenant of capitalism.' Exaggerated as such labels may have been, they designated something real. There were in Europe and there are now in America pacifists and socialists who always support their own government in its international confrontations when push comes to shove."

In other words, what Lynd is saying, and it got much of its impact because it took place within the movement itself, was that, when you come right down to it, the coalitionist policies and the policies of support to the lesser evil aren't merely disagreements among those who want to stop the war in Vietnam, who want to see power eventually go from the hands of the capitalists to the workers and Negroes in this country, but actually disagreements between people on two sides of the barricades, that is, between those who oppose and those who always support their own governments, their own bourgeois governments, in confrontations when push comes to shove. In saying this, Lynd opened up the public rejection of coalitionism, rejecting the entire pattern, strategy, and tactics of Rustin and all those who followed the pattern that Rustin put forth.

It's probably worth stopping now and looking at coalitionism. Actually this discussion took place a year ago, before the election. It was written about and discussed especially in the press of the Young Socialist Alliance and the Socialist Workers Party. Lynd puts his finger on the basic fallacy of coalitionism when he points out that Rustin exaggerates the capacities of the Johnson coalition, of the Democratic Party, to solve the basic social problems which radicals, Negroes, antiwar activists, and class-conscious workers are aware of. This is for a very simple reason.

It's not an individual, such as Johnson, nor even a party, such as the Democratic Party, that's the root of the problem. The root of the problem is the general crisis of liberalism and the general incapacity of American capitalism to solve the problems they find themselves in—or, more accurately, keep creating—in the world today. This got its sharpest attention in the last election with comments on the general drift to the right that has occurred in American foreign policy in the last twenty years. The problem is not whether the Democrats are to the left of the Republicans or whether the Republicans are to the left of the Democrats, but the fact that both of them, as administrators of American capitalism, have seen their policies steadily and surely, in the colonial world and in international confrontations, drift to the right. Within this framework they tactically disagree with one another.

As long as the so-called progressive politicians of these parties stick to liberalism, they can't possibly explain the losses they sustain on the international scene. They can't explain the Chinas; they can't explain the Cubas; they can't even explain the Vietnams. They can't stand up and say, "Well, the problem is simply that we're supporting, for our own interests, the landlord *comprador* regime that's against the interests of the Vietnamese people, and because of this they're fighting, and will fight until we annihilate them, or until they drive us out." It would hardly be a popular statement of policy for a Democrat to make.

So they state that the problem in Vietnam is a problem of infiltration, a problem of the communists. Then the right wing really picks this up and carries it to its logical conclusion. Maybe the best way to understand it is to go back to the phrase that was used so often: "Johnson has carried out Goldwater's policy." The key is, it's not Johnson that's carrying out Goldwater's policy, because the policy is not Goldwater's. The policy is the policy of maintaining control in Southeast Asia, and it would be carried out by either party or by any party that is based on the interests of the American rulers.

In fact, if you want to carry this lesser evil policy to its logical extreme, what the radical movement, what the socialist movement, should have done in the last election was start a big "Draft Eisenhower" campaign, a big third-party Eisenhower movement, because if you sit back and look at the sequence of the Eisenhower administration in Vietnam, the Kennedy administration in Vietnam, and the Johnson administration in Vietnam, there's little question that the good general is the least evil among the three. Merely stating the question that way shows the fallacy of trying to deal with it on the level of the individual bourgeois candidate or even the individual bourgeois party.

But even having said all this, there remains the argument of the coalitionists about benefits, pressures, and reforms in the short run. One variant of this argument I heard presented by David McReynolds at a Militant Labor Forum on September 17. As part of his argument for coalitionism—after basically agreeing with the outline I've just given about the ultimate fallacy, and the ultimate aid that coalitionism gives to the drift to the right and the drift away from working class and Negro politics—McReynolds pointed out that, nevertheless, there's an important bonus that coalitionists get. That's the bonus of being able to pressure and frighten the president at certain periods. He stood up before an audience of about a hundred people, including many militant Negroes, and said, "This is most easily seen if one stops and thinks, what Negro figure is it that was most dangerous to the administration, that they were most concerned about and that they had to take most into their calculations in establishing their basic policy?" He looked around the room and said, "It is, of course, Bayard Rustin." Then he went on blithely about how Rustin's being inside the liberal coalition enables him to act as a tool or pressure hammer against Johnson. Well, I know what I thought, and I found out later that almost everyone else in the room was thinking the same thing: "Yeah, that's the reason why Malcolm X is dead today and Bayard Rustin is able to carry on *his* policies."

I might mention in passing that I think [Conservative Party New York City mayoral candidate] William Buckley understands this whole thing better than the left-wing coalitionists do. To the degree they're even going to talk about pressure, the only pressure comes from independent action that takes away any guaranteed hip-pocket votes. Because here you come to the crux of the problem. Even if you are going to talk in the short-run reformist sense of how do you maximize the reforms that an imperialist government is going to give to you, the last vote that the Democrats have to worry about is the Negro vote and the labor vote. That's the vote they've got in their hip pocket. That's the vote that they can guarantee by merely turning and pointing to the Goldwaters or the Nixons, putting the tag "greater evil, more anti-Negro, more antilabor" on them, and then carry out their real policies.

What happens is that today's greater evil becomes tomorrow's lesser evil, as when the Communist Party writes editorials or the labor bureaucracy writes editorials supporting the great liberal Kefauver against the candidate of the southern governors, Stevenson. And then it's the great liberal Stevenson who must be nominated against the candidate of New England big business, Kennedy. And then it's the great liberal Kennedy who must be supported against the southerners' candidate, Johnson. Then, of course, it's Johnson that must be elected to avoid getting Goldwater.

The result is quite simple: After thirty years of coalitionism as the standard fare, after thirty years of voting for the Democratic Party under the guise of getting something out of it, American labor, the American Negro people, American antiwar activists find themselves in a framework, as far as politics is concerned, that's to the right of where they started from.

Lynd, in his attack on Rustin, doesn't simply end with this rejection of coalitionism. He doesn't restrict himself to the antiwar movement or to the current civil rights movement, and Rustin's similar actions there. He points out the logical conclusion of following coalitionism and adds the following: "The effect of his advice," that is, Rustin's advice, "would be to assimilate Negro [and antiwar] protests to the Establishment [that's the New Left's word for the ruling class], just as the labor protest was co-opted at the end of the 1930's." In other words, Staughton Lynd says that if you want to understand coalitionism, push it back to its beginning, to the 1930s, when modern-day coalitionism, the Democratic Party coalition, as we know it and read about it, was formed.

It is only by seeing the character of the 1930s and the big social movement of the 1930s, which was built around the rise of industrial unionism in this country, that you can understand what coalitionism really is today, what it has grown up to be and what role it plays. The first thing to point out is that the building of the CIO was not just the building of a union movement. It was the building of a great social movement that embraced millions of American workers and their families who had never before been active in political life, in any meaningful way, either on the economic, political, or social front. Industrial unionism, which only a few years before had been considered a utopia, embraced millions before the war began. It was the crisis of the 1930s which undoubtedly produced the CIO, that is, it prepared the conditions for the tumultuous development of industrial unionism. The CIO was not a union of the traditional type known in America, that is, a craft union with conservative, special interests. It began and was organized as a broad class movement based on the factory workers.

In fact, it was a semipolitical movement with profound revolutionary implications. If we look at it correctly, we can say that the CIO, from the moment it began to take mass form, was an incipient or potential labor party, political party of labor, in itself. Thus, as millions flocked into the CIO and as millions made up this social movement in the thirties, the central political question in American politics became: Would the workers, who in unprecedented numbers and with unprecedented speed and combativity had organized themselves as a class on the economic front, would they be capable and would they find the leadership to organize politically as a class, to carry out the fight on the political arena; and eventually, within whatever framework this political movement developed, would the workers then develop a program capable of replacing capitalism with socialism, replacing the capitalist parties' rule with their rule? Not only was this the key question for the workers and for the great social movement in the thirties, it was of course the key question for the capitalists in this country, who, under the leadership of Roosevelt, attempted to adjust, reshape, and reform the institutions of rule in order to absorb the discontent and the upsurge into the traditional political forms.

In 1936, the leaders of the CIO, backed up by the leaders of the Communist Party and many in the Socialist Party, supported Roosevelt. They urged support for the Democratic Party and established for the first time the labor-Negro-liberal Democratic Party coalition. These leaders had no real perspective of independent political action by the workers themselves. They had a perspective of reform and pressure, not education and preparation for revolutionary change.

Before going any further, we might start cleaning up the language about coalitionism, the Democratic Party, labor, et cetera. That is, when you talk about the Democratic Party, or read someone discussing the Democratic Party, as a labor-Negro-liberal coalition—and when you include the great mass of the American workers in it—you are not really talking about a party membership, you are talking about a voting bloc, an electoral weight. That is, the average worker, the average Negro, who once every four years or once every two years pulls the Democratic lever, is a voter, not a party member. He plays no role, he takes no daily part in, and he knows damned little about the Democratic Party.

This is very important, because it brings more sharply into focus the basic idea that a political party's policy is determined not by who pulls the lever for it every four years. The party is defined and determined by the program it puts forth and by what set of policies and strategies in the world and at home it puts forth, and what class or group within a class these policies serve.

The class the party votes for in its program and policies, not the party that the class votes for, is what determines the kind of party it is. By this criterion the Democratic Party in the 1930s and 1940s was, and remains today, a bourgeois party, a party whose basic program is in the interests of the American ruling class. The electoral coalition forged by Franklin Delano Roosevelt, by the CIO heads, and by the Communist Party, merely guaranteed a solid constituency, to use a term in common usage, at least for a brief period of time.

What we are really talking about when we use the phrase American labor-Negro-liberal coalition is a coalition between the owners of American industry and finance and, on the one hand, the professional ward-heelers and politicians who keep the party machinery oiled, and, on the other hand, the various trade union bureaucrats and leaders of protest movements in American society, whose job it is to bring out the ranks of the coalition at voting time to guarantee the continuance of the rule of this party as opposed to the Republican Party. They are the safety factor, they are the insurance policy, because when the general propaganda fails, when someone starts to step out of line, when the candidates of the party get to be a little too much to stomach, it's those boys who whip things into shape, who go to the workers, to the Negroes, to the socialists, and say, "Look, it's in your class interests, it's in your interests as socialists, to come out and vote for this group, as a tactic"—in order, of course, to defeat the "greater evil."

Now that we've separated the electoral votes, the coalition, and the party, which are quite different entities, we can answer the most basic question: Who really needs this coalition? If you stop to think about it for a moment, it is crystal clear that the small minority who manage to maintain their rule through this coalition—the American capitalist class—are the ones who need the coalition.

When David McReynolds debated Peter Camejo a few weeks ago at the forum I referred to earlier, McReynolds kept emphasizing how badly the Negroes need allies, how badly the workers need allies, how badly the antiwar activists need allies, how they are all small minorities. He kept forgetting to mention the smallest minority of them all—the tiny clique that rules this country through the Democratic Party. They are the ones who are desperate for allies, because they are the ones who, if it depended on their own numbers, could never put anyone in power. In fact, they wouldn't get nearly as many votes as [New York City SWP mayoral candidate] Clifton DeBerry is going to get next week on election day. If they lost the voting bloc every election day, they would have to find a new way of ruling, a new way of fooling people, or step from the scene. The final argument of coalitionism—the alleged weakness of the American workers and their alleged need for this coalition—stands everything ultimately completely on its head, because they are the last ones who need the coalition; the coalition is what keeps the American ruling class in power.

Just as the major task, the central question, of the 1930s was whether the working class would build a political arm, so the major concern, the major task, of the politicians who serve this minority capitalist class today is to prevent the majority class from organizing itself as an independent political force and destroying this coalition.

Of course, as far as revolutionary socialists are concerned, the key becomes the break-up and destruction of this coalition and the winning over of the mass of the Negroes, the workers, the radicalized students, and the dissatisfied middle class to a new platform, a new program, and opening their eyes to the character of the leadership that has tied them to this capitalist party.

I want to read to you the final rebuttal in this whole argument between the coalitionists, as represented by Rustin, and the anticoalitionists, as represented partially by Lynd. While Lynd rejected coalitionism, he had nothing viable to offer as an alternative. But I'm including him because he was the prime example of the rejection of the path of coalitionism.

The reply to this entire debate and this attack on Rustin and coalitionism within the antiwar movement came, interestingly and appropriately enough, not from Rustin, who couldn't have cared less because that's not where his constituency comes from. It came from the coalitionist wing of SDS, from its most prominent spokesmen, Steve Max and Douglas Ireland, in a long article attacking Staughton Lynd and defending Bayard Rustin.

THE DEMOCRATIC PARTY COALITION / 71

It's an article of about fourteen pages, which I can't go into in detail. But now that we've clarified this question of coalition, electoral bloc, and party, I want to read to you their key paragraph that summarized the best and most complete answer from the coalitionist side. They say: "In 1964 Lyndon Johnson led a conscious anti-Goldwater coalition, including labor, Negroes, ethnic minorities, liberals, intellectuals, some elements of big business, some Dixiecrats [*some* Dixiecrats—like you'll find *some* milk in a cow's udder], reform Democrats, machine Democrats, professional elements, and liberal Republicans. Of these elements, the Negroes, the trade unions, the churches, and the liberals and intellectuals were the most progressive and dynamic. This coalition had a common purpose, the defeat of Goldwater. [Listen to this logic now.] But the moment the election was won the Johnson coalition objectively became the Johnson party, an arena in which these various forces contend for political power and influence. In terms of national politics, it is in this arena that we, like Rustin, see the elements for a new political coalition of the more advanced forces that built the 1964 coalition."

So they take the entire thing and they stand it right on its head.

Of course it was a conscious anti-Goldwater coalition. Every four years it's a conscious anti-some Republican coalition. Naturally once the election was over, the fight took place inside the party. But that's the place where the labor-Negro-liberal elements are not located. That's the place where the majority of the people have no say. And of course three years from now, after the struggle for hegemony in the imaginary coalition, once more a conscious anti-Republican campaign will be run and the same forces will be urged to support it for the same reasons—in order to "strengthen" themselves, the better to fight, after their real interests have been defeated.

This was the path that Lynd rejected. But the rejection itself is not the solution. Without the rejection of participation and work within the Democratic Party, no steps forward can be taken. But rejection is only the first step.

The term *independent political action*, unfortunately, almost like the term *peace*, is very abstract and very algebraic. You know, just think of the word *peace* for a moment. Lyndon Johnson is for peace; everyone is for peace. In fact, the more they slug it out the more they are for peace. In some ways, the term *independent political action* is almost the same.

Walk up to almost anyone on the street and ask, "Do you want to be independent politically or dependent politically?" They'll say, "Independent." To put any meaning, any concrete meaning in the formula independent political action, we have to go back to the basic question I discussed earlier, the class character of the party. The Democratic Party carries out the policies and the needs of the American capitalist class; this defines its basic character. If we are going to talk about independent political action, we have to begin to define it as independent of this party *and* the class it serves. In other words, stop talking about independent political action and start talking about independent working class political action, or independent socialist political action.

This is important because the entire question cannot be separated from the electoral arena, as I've shown. The major fallacy is that there is a way to outsmart and outwit the Democratic Party. These people say they are not really coalitionists but it's a tactical question whether they are in or out. But it always ends up the same way. At the same time, the question is certainly not isolated to the electoral arena.

This is another common fallacy: When revolutionary Marxists put forth the concept of independent political action, they are merely talking about their own election campaigns every couple of years. That's totally false. For revolutionists, education, propaganda, and agitation for working class political action, for a labor party, for a socialist party, for a break with capitalist politics is part and parcel of the struggle against the Meanys and Reuthers, the Rustins and Kings, the Thomases, the Harringtons, the anonymous editorial writers of the *Worker*.

The mere algebraic call for some form of independent political action still leaves the door open back to coalitionism. There are many examples of this. The easiest way to put it is: The call and the demand and the insistence on independent labor political action, and independent socialist political action, are part and parcel of the struggle against the leaders and privileged layers of the working class, the trade union movement, the civil rights organizations, whose very existence is tied up with the maintenance of this coalition and the maintenance of dependence. And they will go an awful long way to salvage this when they have to.

One of the best examples of this was the American Labor Party in New York. I don't have time to go into it in detail. But when the Social Democratic fakers in New York were faced with the problem that a lot of their workers still hadn't become "sophisticated" enough to understand they were supposed to vote for capitalist politicians in 1936, they formed a labor party, the American Labor Party. That's independent political action, isn't it? It had one small twist—it voted for Roosevelt. In other words, there's more than one way to prevent the establishment of real independent politics. There have been many other examples in the so-called reform movements. The Progressive Party in 1948 is a very educational example of this. But that's a topic for later on.

Thus these forms of so-called independent politics—the American Labor Party forms, the forms of uniting with the existing leaderships of these movements for a "socialist" program—are steps right back to coalitionism through the back door. And what this does is to bring us back to where we started. That is, to the antiwar activists, to these new radicals whose actions have thrown this question once again to the fore in the last few months.

I don't call them the New Left or a New Left. Because they are not this. This is one of the misused and abused terms. What they actually are and what we actually see in front of us is a new layer of radicals. A small but significant and growing radicalization in American society. A layer whose political physiognomy is not yet determined in any significant way. What is important about their current activity—other than the fact that it is a protest which is almost unique in American society: against a war while that war is still going on—is the fact that their demand to bring the troops home is a confrontation with Johnson and with this entire layer of coalitionists, and that threatens the coalition. Their mere existence and their mere refusal to compromise threatens this coalition. This explains not only the attacks they receive from the press and from the government, but the vicious and now unanimous attacks that the leaders of American labor have come out with against antiwar demonstrators.

Their problem is not a rejection or an acceptance of an Old Left—again an imaginary, false, homogeneous concept—but understanding how to reject the reform-pressure-coalition perspective that the Communist and Socialist parties developed to a fine art from the thirties on, in place of a program of revolutionary opposition to the Democratic Party and its allies. That is, the program that the revolutionary socialists fought for in the 1930s, in the 1940s, in the 1950s, and that we still fight for today.

What they don't need is an American Labor Party, Progressive Party, Community Party, Peace Party back-door path back to coalitionism. But education and organization for socialism to understand the need for class independence and for no compromises with the defenders of coalition. In other words, we need to win, recruit, and train out of this layer not more Reuthers but more revolutionists.

It is very important that this layer of young radicals understand that first and foremost what determines the character of any organization's politics, what's most basic of all, is the program. There is no shortcut, there is no easy way around establishing a set of principles and a set of demands and an approach, and there is no way around the fact that these will be in the interests of one layer of society—one class—or another. They must recognize what they must be after, that is, the abolition of capitalism, for it doesn't make much difference how big a party or how big a constituency they form, it'll have the same results. I'm always struck by this fallacy, the big number fallacy. The idea that, in essence, first you draw together the people and then later you tell them what the program really is, or later they discover what the program really is. I think we have had our best example of the horrendous effect that such an approach can have in Indonesia the last couple of months.

Here was an organization, the Indonesian Communist Party, that claimed three million members; three million members in its youth group; and a following of over twenty million in the mass organizations of the workers, peasants, women, students, and government employees that it led. And it is currently undergoing an utter annihilation at the hands of an army of about 350,000. The problem of the Indonesian Communist Party is not its constituency. It's hard to imagine a much bigger constituency for any radical party, as a percentage of the toiling population. The problem is, you can't turn a sponge into a sword overnight, no matter how large the sponge is.

Let's say you are worried about burglars in your house. Some guy comes along and says, here is a giant Saint Bernard. He weighs about 200 pounds, and anyone who would come into your apartment with that dog there is crazy. So you take him and you pet him, teach him to compromise, teach him that anyone who comes in the door is OK. So you're sitting there one night and someone pops in the door—a burglar. You tell the dog, "Get him! Get him!" The 200 pounds doesn't do him a damn bit of good. In fact, he's most likely to run interference for the burglar.

If the time is not yet ripe, if there aren't a lot of Saint Bernards willing and ready to be trained, you'd be much better off to get yourself a small, wiry terrier that weighs about ten pounds. Then train him, make him crystal clear, make him antiburglar to the core, so if the time comes when you can find a Saint Bernard, at least the Saint Bernard will have an example to follow.

I'll end by saying that it is important to remember that the objective pace of events cannot be forced. None of us in this room can, nor does any of us pretend we can, force the pace and development of the radicalization of the American working class. That's in hands much more subversive than ours, the hands of the American ruling class, to take care of over time.

But what we can do, and what our major responsibility is, and what the major debate among us is about, is the program and organization that we present to the layer of radicals that does exist and is growing—whether they'll enter the mass movements of the future with reformist or with revolutionary perspectives.

STANLEY ARONOWITZ: I'm grateful to Jack Barnes for having dealt such decisive blows to the position of Bayard Rustin. He's saved me about fifteen minutes and, I suspect, you as well.

In 1917 there was another war, and a socialist ran for mayor of New York; his name was Morris Hillquit, later to be maligned by all sorts of radicals as a hopeless Social Democrat and a betrayer of the working class. Hillquit took the position in 1917 that the First World War was an imperialist war. He ran for mayor on the program of "Don't

Send the Boys." Throughout the entire city of New York, Hillquit spoke against the war, characterizing it in class terms as an instrument of American capitalist expansion, and 40,000 people, so the stories go, followed Hillquit from street corner to street corner, and he never had fewer than 15,000 or 20,000 people with him as he made speeches night after night against the war.

The greatest socialist of them all, Eugene V. Debs, stood on a corner in Canton, Ohio, and told Canton steelworkers that they should not go and fight. And Debs in 1918 stood trial, a political trial that received a hell of a lot of publicity, and served his jail term until 1920, when Warren Harding released him from jail, but not before he got one million votes on a socialist program, as a vindication of his antiwar position.

The Socialist Party, up until 1920, rejected the notion of coalition. It refused systematically the attempts of the Teddy Roosevelt Progressives, of the Wilsons, of even the people in Illinois around John Peter Altgeld, to co-opt the tremendous socialist strength throughout this country into a political coalition with the Democrats or with the Republican national leaders. In Milwaukee, the Socialists took the mayor's seat and then sent Victor Berger to Congress. On the local level, here on the Lower East Side, where we are sitting now, Meyer London was sent to Congress and stood up in 1917 and voted against the war credits. And out he went, but not before the American Congress was forced to reveal the true nature of this war and the fact that in the wake of systematic electoral opposition to that war the American government was not about to permit an elected representative of the people to sit in that Congress and express his views.

The thing about the Socialist Party, up until 1920, was that it was a mass party. And it was a very interesting kind of party. It was a party that had in it left-wingers. I believe that, with the exception of the Industrial Workers of the

World, who took a syndicalist position—that the workers should take over the factories and not worry about electoral politics—that the Socialists were hopelessly electorally oriented. With the exception of some anarchists who were really part of the radical community then and quite significant in some ways, most of the leaders of the left wing of the radical movement in this country were in the Socialist Party: James Cannon, who founded American Trotskyism; Charles Ruthenberg, one of the founders of the American Communist Party; John Reed, who popularized the Bolshevik revolution; and many important trade union leaders.

The reason I'm going through this is, we had a very important object lesson from the history of American radicalism, which I think we must bring to this discussion. Prior to the Bolshevik revolution, when the real problem that Americans were addressing themselves to was the problem of how to defeat their own corporate leaders, and when there was never any doubt in the socialist movement who the enemy was, it was possible for a left which took a firm, revolutionary anti-imperialist position throughout the entire period and a center which didn't take such a firm position but was never really in doubt about who the enemy was and what they had to do—people like Hillquit—it was possible for them to coalesce in the same political party.

There was a very good reason why this coalition was possible. The reason was that they had fundamental agreement on a program. And they had fundamental agreement on an ideology. And it was not disagreements on tactics of achieving socialism or tactics of achieving a broad anti-imperialist movement in this country that determined where they went and in what slots they found themselves. It was the fact that they understood the prime character of American imperialism as a rapacious imperialism, as the dominant feature of American capitalism in the early 1900s, and as the central problem that socialists had to address themselves to.

They understood that fact, and therefore it was possible for a Hillquit to get united support in New York City for a campaign that had enormous strength and got over 200,000 votes in 1917.

We are now in a period which is not at all in some ways similar to 1917, nor is it similar to 1920 when Debs ran for president. But we are in a period, and I think Barnes put this very well, where we are once again raising the question. Because the tremendous power of the antiwar movement—not to change the policy of our government, because we are not about to change policies of our government, no matter what the hell we do, based on our present strength—plus the power and disillusionment of the Negro freedom movement have raised the question: Where do we go from here? . . .

Now in New York and around the country on October 15 and 16 we began to answer coalition in a new way: Based on our agreement that the war in Vietnam was a crock and we had to get out of it, based on our general agreement that the enemy lay specifically and concretely with the government policy in that area, we found a measure of unity around a slogan: "Stop the War in Vietnam Now!"

That kind of coalition begins to parallel the beginnings of the coalition that existed within the Socialist Party. That is, we defined a program, we defined a direction, and we were able to find minimum areas of agreement while maintaining our organizational discretion. Nobody said, we are forming a new coalition, an umbrella of organizations; we said, we are going into a specific action on a specific basis and this has been developed on a national level by the National Coordinating Committee to End the War in Vietnam.

Now this is our answer to the way in which Rustin and Company pose the question of coalition. Rustin starts from a very broad historical perspective. A perspective which abstractly and, from the point of view, I suspect, of history, may have some objective—whatever that word means—validity.

That is, he says, "I'm for a radical political movement too, but if you don't have the workers, and you don't have the masses of the Negro people, and if you don't have the intellectuals, in other words, if you are not in the mainstream of American life, these are sectarian movements." The basic strategy for radicals therefore ought to be to go into these movements that form the base of the Democratic Party and transform them into radical movements.

He has told us—the left, whether it's the New Left, the Old Left, or whatever you want to call it—to abandon the sharp cutting edge of our position and of our critique of current political questions. He has told us to stop organizing independently outside of this coalition and to attempt to influence it from the inside. As if what Art Preis told us in *Labor's Giant Step* never happened—which was that the Communist Party, the Socialist Party, and practically everybody else on the left went into the labor movement, organized for John L. Lewis, and then Lewis promptly kicked them out. And when John L. Lewis was unable to kick them out, Harry Truman and Phil Murray finished the job in 1948.

So he wants us to go through and repeat the same process. Well, we are not prepared to relive history, and therefore to a large degree the radical impulses behind the Negro freedom movement and the radical impulses in the antiwar movement are not about to join in Johnson's or anybody else's liberal coalition.

But the real question is what do we do as an alternative? I would like to say what I think some of the ideological elements at the root of coalition politics are. The first root of coalition is based on the doctrine that every college student has had to study in Political Science I, the doctrine of democratic pluralism, a theory by which we understand American politics to be the confluence of pressure groups acting on a vortex in a kind of physical way which somehow, as a result of the stresses and strains of those pressures, results in, evolves a policy. That is, there is the corporate pressure group, there is the labor pressure group, there is the Negro pressure group, there is the liberal pressure group, there are those for artificial insemination—they're a pressure group—there is the Planned Parenthood Association, which is the other side of artificial insemination—they're a pressure group; and all these groups sort of fight it out in the marketplace of ideas.

Corresponding to that kind of confluence of pressures we finally get a policy. And there are ideologists like Seymour Martin Lipset, who does not deny the nature of classes and the operation of classes in the basic direction of American politics. All he says is that since we have a great amount of material resources in this country and since capitalism has been able to solve the problem of scarcity, the question that we now have to address is not, who controls scarce means, but instead, who is going to get a larger share of the enormous pie. Not the question of ownership and control, which is essentially a socialist position, but the question of how do we bite into that pie so that we get more. And in doing so, he has reiterated what Samuel Gompers, the first head of the American Federation of Labor, said a long time ago: "What labor wants is more." And what do you want after that, he was asked. "More!" he said.

Now there are a number of radicals who, in essence, although not in appearance, have in the past acted as if they rejected the whole notion of class politics, or the whole notion of the class basis of control and rule in this country. And all they want is to get more. They can be as exercised about any given government policy as you want, but until they raise the question of who controls, who owns, where the power lies—what Paul Potter said at the April 17 march: "Who is our enemy?"—they remain participants in the great myth of democratic pluralism. And that's what lies in part behind what Rustin talks about as the liberal coalition which he wants us to participate in and to lead eventually.

The real problem there is that the second ideological basis of Rustin's position is also accepted by most radicals, and that is that we have substantial agreement about how we play politics. Anytime you accept the notion of democratic pluralism in effect and you see nothing basically wrong with the society or the way in which it operates on you, then you have to only criticize. No matter how many draft cards you burn, no matter how many picket lines and sit-ins and lunch-ins and all the rest of it you participate in, you're always in the position of only being able to criticize a policy, and never seeing its connection with other policies and with the system.

Therefore most people in the peace movement today criticize Johnson's policy in Vietnam but reject the concept that somehow that policy is part of a general relationship with other policies in our society—not only in the whole area of foreign policy, which some of us call neocolonialism or imperialism, but also its relationship with the kind of needs that people have on a day-to-day basis in terms of the welfare state.

So what we end up with is a fragmented movement, a movement with no serious impact, because it never raises what is really the fundamental question that any movement needs to raise in order to be truly political. And that is the question of power, who controls. Those are the issues that movements need to develop, and what is happening now is that the Rustins and the rest of them are putting forth their views to our movements. When I use the word *our movements*, I mean the movements of radical insurgency, because what they are trying to prevent is a new coalition, a coalition based on a program which raises the question of power, and they are trying to keep the movement as pressure groups so that they can participate in this myth of democratic pluralism and therefore be co-opted into the Johnson coalition.

Now I think we as radicals have to get away from the box that we have been put into. The question that we have been asked today is kind of a false question, though I think everybody knows what it means. I'm not being critical of the conference organizers for posing it because this is the way it's put popularly. It's not coalition we are opposed to. You see, we are not in a position now as radicals to go into a coalition with the liberals, for one fundamental reason—except on a very specific kind of issue like a parade or a civil rights demonstration—because we bring to that coalition only one thing now. We bring, as radicals, only our organizing talent, and in certain sections of the left our money and our intelligence.

What they bring is power, and they bring ideologically, although not physically very often, the line that we have to organize under. Such as the situation in the SANE November 27 parade, for example, where we are now being asked to march under their banner, under their slogans, to Washington to protest the war. They want a coalition with radical peace groups, or radical political parties, but they don't want us to speak, and they don't want us to really be on their sponsoring list, and they don't really want to work out that program with us, but they want us there. Because they know that we know how to organize and that we have certain basic contacts, and they know that there is a new constituency, if you'll excuse the word, Jack, that they have to win in order to have an impressive demonstration for themselves. That is the student constituency, and possibly some new elements in the civil rights constituency, and they may or may not get them, but we have to understand what we are in when we do things like that.

We have no base for radical ideas in this country, so therefore there is no radical movement. There are radical organizers, radical ideologists, radical speakers, radical activists, but there isn't a radical movement because there is nobody in this country yet in the masses that responds to the whole question of a fundamental critique of American society and makes the connection between the cold war as the dominant fact of American life in the forties, fifties, and sixties and everything else that American society is about.

We have no following, except maybe a couple of thousand students, for the concept that it is the war machine that frustrates the housing program, that it is the racist war machine that makes it possible in part for the continuance of the ghetto, that it is the war machine that puts the 3.2 percent wage freeze on workers. We really don't have that kind of following for that kind of position. And therefore I come to the conclusion that if we are going to be true to our radical position, and true to the energies that we have exhibited and fantastically been able to bring to the antiwar movement, to the civil rights movement, and historically to movements like the labor movement and youth movement generally, we must consciously build a radical political base in this country.

That is really the task now. A radical political base is not radicals organizing generally around the issue of voter registration, and it's not organizing only against the war in Vietnam. A radical political base is going into the communities, going into the shops, going onto the campus, around the position—that, I think, to a large degree Barnes and I could agree with—that corporations control the whole range of U.S. policy and that the basic issue we face is who runs the policy and the program, for what purposes and in whose interests are wars, racist violence, bad housing, and bad schools maintained. The reason we have to do that is not because we have any immediate chances of success, but because that is the only way in which we are going to prevent the co-optators, the coalitionists of the right, from taking us in.

If we develop our own position, and try to translate that into a mass movement, and then develop a mass movement somewhere along the line around key programmatic demands that we can spell out in a second, then when we come into the coalitions with the liberals around specific issues, we are in a much different position. And that's what the students have just about begun to nibble at.

What we are now are radical gadflies. There is now a committee for the reexamination of Far East policy alternatives. The reason that committee was established is that Humphrey and Johnson need a committee, they need a committee that they can pretty much control and that they can attract all kinds of sentiment to. Well, the only reason that committee was established, is that we have had October 15 and 16, because there was an April March on Washington, because we had a radical political cutting edge that forced the liberals into action. We have to welcome the fact that the liberals are in action, because the liberal actions really reflect the fact that we have to a certain extent in the antiwar movement developed the initiative. We have the initiative now. But to the extent that we do not maintain that impetus, that momentum, and build ourselves a political base that goes beyond students, that goes beyond lower middle class people, that goes among workers and Negroes particularly—and I think that we are in full agreement on where the power for an alternative lies—to that extent we will lose the initiative and find ourselves back where we are.

Considering where we were before April 17 in the antiwar movement or where we are now in the civil rights movement, important changes have been made, because to a certain extent some of the better organizations in the civil rights movement failed to make the leap. But where they did—in Mississippi—even though they called themselves the Freedom Democratic Party, because they opposed the administration they were able to send waves through the entire liberal establishment.

People are asking the question: What are we going to do?

I think we have to raise the question of independent politics. Not in the way that the American Labor Party did, not in the way that says that we now must endorse a reform Democrat and give them another line on the ballot, or we have to endorse Johnson and give him another line, but on the basis of the central idea that the cold war and the corporations are responsible for our frustrations, not only in foreign policy but on domestic issues. We have to raise a new element that radicals have never raised in that program.

You see, we have missed the big boat that only the Socialists before 1920 understood: that the real political issue that radicalizes people is not more housing, is not higher wages, is not another school in the community. That just brings people into the system and strengthens the system of domination. But if that victory is conducted on the basis of a fight for democratic control, which in England people raise as the fight for workers' control, if we begin to move with people on the question that they can run their government, that they have the right to a say in policy, that they must be consulted, and that they must determine the direction of American foreign policy before they can accept any political leadership—if that becomes the key, then it is very difficult to win that, because the whole meaning of the welfare system, which Barnes talks about in terms of the CIO, was the ability of the establishment to develop a big breast for the American working class, which was called benefits, cradle-to-grave benefits.

It was a weakened example of what went on in Germany that co-opted the German workers, that has gone on in England that brought the English workers very close into the system. Now you can't oppose welfare, and you can't support welfare unless you raise the question of who controls the welfare system, where does the control lie.

Radicals have been historically elitist, elitist in this sense: that they think the whole thing is on the external level, the level of ideology, the level of opposition, the level of fixed programs. By the way, I'm not being critical of the SWP alone in this kind of analysis. But I am being critical of every radical movement since the old Socialist Party. By the way, you should read the old Socialist stuff; it is a marvel of democratic socialism of the left and democratic socialism of the right. But the point was that people were beginning to think of the practical problems of how they are going to run the government. They raised socialist issues, except for the municipalities, where they became gas and water socialists who went right down the drain with the sewer. They began to raise the question of who had the right to govern.

Now it seems to me that to project an independent political alternative on a national, ideological level—by that I mean with the alternative of socialism, with the projection of a radical political party that contests for national office—is nice but it does not meet the fundamental problem that we have to address ourselves to, which is, how do we build a base, how do we get a following for some key concepts which I hope I have outlined.

I don't think you can do it nationally, not because I don't think it's possible, because the problems of consciousness are not there, but because our resources, what we can bring to such an effort, would make that kind of thing meaningless.

What we can do on the local level is begin to project this kind of perspective not only on the basis of electoral action, but on the basis of trying to combine the community organizing efforts that SNCC and SDS and a number of other organizations pioneered in the sixties with the idea of the electoral alternative. Not the arid electoral campaign or candidate which we've been used to, running around elections and organizing around elections alone, but utilizing elections for the educational purpose of understanding American neocolonialism and understanding the alternative in terms of socialism, and utilizing the day-to-day organizing around rent strikes, problems of control, various programs, educational forums, and discussions, utilizing those things to build a popular following for certain ideas.

That really is what we have to do. I think that the radicals, most of us, in effect have come to the conclusion that that task is impossible. That we are not able to go into the Lower East Side or the West Side or Philadelphia or Chicago or Detroit, and build a popular political following, a club and an organization in the community where our parties or our political movements have a real community base. We say that we have to build mass movements of a pressure group nature—and by the way, those will continue and I endorse them, because they do bring people into activity—and then take people from those movements and bring them over here to political action. I think that says that we don't have enough confidence in our own ability to project a program and to develop a program on a political level, an honest political level on a community basis.

I think that has to be altered. I think that's what the Freedom Democratic Party began to alter. I think in New York that we cannot come to the voters once every two years, or once every year. We have to come to the community on a day-by-day basis, and that's the only way we are ever going to get a following. Otherwise we are going to find ourselves fighting within coalition organizations for the rest of our lives.

I'm hesitant to use the word socialism—though not shamefaced, I'm a socialist—because I think that we have to bring the socialist content and not simply the socialist slogan to people. What do I mean by socialist content? The most subversive idea in this country is that the people of this country have the right to own and control their own government, their own society, their own industry. The most subversive idea is not when you get more welfare benefits, but when you raise the question of us and not them that has got to be in the saddle. The most subversive idea is that we have to define new forms of guaranteeing mass popular participation in the whole political process. And we have to define those forms not in abstract electoral or political senses, but in terms of the economic system, in terms of the welfare system, all places where people are impinged upon by this society, where they are oppressed.

Speaking as a trade unionist—in my own work as an organizer that is what I do—I try to convince people that they have a right to run that shop somewhere down the road, and that their whole thing is not whether the boss is going to give them money, because in the chemical industry, the boss is always ready to give them money. He's always talking about wages: we will give you wages, we will give you fringe benefits, we will give you every type of better pension plan you want—just don't ask us to put a section into the contract that gives you the right to veto the introduction of new machinery into the plant. Don't question our right to manage the shop. . . .

What we have to understand, at least what I've come to understand through my experience, is that we are dealing with a very powerful capitalist society. It's a society that cannot stop its general crisis. That is, it can't stop the wars or the tendency to war, and we are in for all sorts of new adventures everywhere. But it is a society that is able to do two things at once, which we never imagined American or any other capitalism able to do: To increase the pace and quantity of social welfare benefits, to increase wages and the standard of living, on the one hand; and to decrease the level of popular control and increase the monopoly control of all of our politics and economic life, on the other.

This is the contradiction that we face in building radical consciousness. How do we raise the issue of socialism or radical alternatives, if our entire thrust is on the basis of material things, that is, issues? Well, I think what we have to understand is that many workers and Negroes are built into the system by virtue of their pensions, their welfare benefits, by the welfare system itself. And that our real problem is to break them ideologically from the political system, and the only way we can do that is by talking about democracy in a new way. That's the basis. Then we have to say that if you really believe in democratic control, you have to have your own political movement.

I don't think we are about to have a socialist movement which runs on a socialist program next week. And I'm not the kind of person who believes with a number of other people that what we've got to do is simply to say, let the people decide.

No, I think that we have to point out the connections between the war system and what is going on in the community. I think we have to introduce this as a political issue. I think we have to run candidates in opposition to those candidates who do not understand the system, and do not organize around that concept. We have to utilize, however, most important, the central notion that without a popular following, coalition is inevitable, absorption of radicals into the liberal coalition is inevitable, and until we, no matter how hard and arduous it may be, really make a serious attempt to attain that radical following, we are up the creek without a paddle.

QUESTIONS

QUESTION: Stanley Aronowitz, do you have criticisms of the early Socialist Party?
ARONOWITZ: ... Am I suggesting that it is a model for the future? The early Socialist Party was narrow in the sense that it adopted a line which recognized only its own alter-

native to capitalism as a real alternative—and particularly the electoral alternative; it was nonrevolutionary in the practical sense as a political party. There were revolutionary tendencies in that party that recognized the possibility of organized revolution, but it did participate in the worldwide Social Democratic reliance on electoral action.

On the other hand, it ruthlessly, but with great reluctance, purged people like Bill Haywood, who came up with syndicalist solutions, and it weakened its working class base because it did not regard a multi-issue kind of political movement as valid except within the electoral alternative. It was also to a large degree anti-ideological. That is, it became very fuzzy because in many stages in its life people who had liberal tendencies operated within it and were able to influence it. Thirdly, the party's rank and file was very often separated from its leadership. The rank and file was working class and the leadership was very often and for a long time middle class.

But its strength was that it permitted organization around the ideas of socialism in the electoral arena to take place. . . . And the Socialist Party understood that the process of radical consciousness was one that moved from liberalism to radicalism and people were not born radicals. The other strength was that it tolerated a large degree of disagreement within its ranks and on the whole, from 1900 to 1920, came up on the right side of the fence. Now I think that where it is a model is that it was a mass party and not a vanguard party. And I think that's what we are going to have to do in this country to have independent radical political action—that is, attempt, no matter how hard it is, to build a mass party.

BARNES: Well, this is a whole subject in itself. I want to look at it from another point of view. You see, the characteristics which Stanley Aronowitz paints of the Socialist Party were not only its strengths, they were also integrally its weaknesses. A heterogeneous party, given the peculiar role that Debs played—that is, as its principal and most articulate revolutionary spokesman—was bound to be busted apart on the shoals of differences when explosive revolutionary events and changes took place internationally and nationally.

The fact that it was a mass party did not prevent this from happening. The first question—not the first question at the time, but the first question if you are going to make a revolution—is not the mass character of the party but the program of the party. Because unless the masses are won to the program that is in their historical interests and not a rigid set of dogmas, the mass doesn't do you any good. Once faced with the crisis of the war and the Russian revolution and the question of power in America and a working class party in American society, plus the prosperity of the twenties, the Socialist Party collapsed. Even though it did all the things you say, it had so many heterogeneous opinions that were all expressed publicly. It had a leader, a central figure with whom the entire party was identified—Debs, who did not understand the connection between the structure and program of the party, or, I don't know which, did not care or think it was important. In spite of this it busted apart. If it hadn't happened when it did following the war, it would have happened later.

So the key lesson the Socialist Party teaches us is that the mass base is not enough. The question is: Does the party have a socialist program—including a transitional concept of how to get to socialism and the type of party that is needed—such that, when it wins a mass base, it can carry out a revolutionary transformation of American society and lead the workers to take governmental power into their own hands? A new kind of party, one like the Bolsheviks, was needed. Without this criterion, the mass base means nothing. Without the mass base the programmatic leadership and membership are doomed to a life as a sterile sect.

But without the program the mass base means nothing. It has no meaning.

Take the Socialist Party in France; take the Communist Party in Italy. Take Sukarno in Indonesia. If you want a mass party of the workers who call themselves communist and talk about power and, I suspect, with quite a range of opinions within it that are expressed, you can't find a better one than that. But it has one fatal flaw: That party has been trained and bred under the watchful eye of Mao—not on the revolutionary struggle for power against the national bourgeoisie in Indonesia, the neocolonial retainers—but on reformism. And, facing a social crisis, this party of six million followers is being crushed.

QUESTION: I want to ask a question about the concrete tactics that Stanley proposed. I understand that Stanley is one of the signers of a statement or proposal for a local New York political organization in one of the congressional districts. I was talking to Jimmy Weinstein the other night, who is also a signer, I believe, and he said that you intended to take part in the Democratic primary as a functional operation. I just wondered if you would comment on that and explain why you want to do that.

ARONOWITZ: First, it is not a proposal for a party, it is a proposal for a political committee. It's called the Committee for Independent Political Action, and it exists.

The idea of the committee is, as Barnes so correctly said, to build a movement around a program and not to build a movement around a constituency. That is, not to say we want to win people in this community, therefore we are going to have a program. In this sense it differs from the Communist Party, but not from the Socialist Party from 1900 to 1920, because they had a program: it was called socialism.

Our program is what we consider to be the central reason that we are an independent and radical political movement.

The program is that the cold war and its Vietnams are what set the tone and pace for all other questions in this country, that the racism that is inherent in our society and in our foreign policy not only limits what kind of domestic issues we can have, what kind of domestic struggles we can carry on—because you can't get any money for anything, including a poverty program—but it also determines the fact that there can be no political democracy in this country as long as the inheritors of the corporate system are in control of our policies. And that is stated openly and publicly.

Now the reason we raise the idea of possibly running in the Democratic primary—and we are not wedded to the idea—is because we regard the form as being a practical question, just as politicians from radical political organizations work in the antiwar movement, even in liberal movements sometimes. All you need is 1,000 signatures and you can enter the Democratic primary. Now in New York City, where most people participate in electoral politics through the primary and not through the general election, we see that it might be possible to run in the primary and then go on and run in the general election.

This is analogous to the view that the Freedom Democratic Party took in Mississippi. That is, the political question in Mississippi was not whether you ran in the Democratic primary, whether you called yourself Democratic or not, but what your program was. Whether you were opposed to the racists in Mississippi or not.

The thing that we want to prevent is setting a sterile limit on the number of arenas that we can participate in. To a large degree, the Republican and Democratic parties in this country represent the same class. And yet they are arenas in which all kinds of opposition can take place, because they are not parties that nominate at the convention. Before Carmine DeSapio made the Democratic primary an open primary, there was no question that third party politics was the only way in which independent politics could be played in this country. Now we are saying that we need an independent political movement that will evolve into a third party. We will attack the Democratic Party, we will attack the Johnson administration, but we will at the same time not shut the door to what we consider to be a meaningful forum. We think that there is a possibility of entering a primary in order to educate people. It's like revolutionaries entering elections because they want to educate people; they don't necessarily believe they are going to win in the elections, or that elections are the way in which people can gain power, but they believe that there is a possibility that there will be people who will listen through such a forum.

We are not calling ourselves the Reform Democratic Party Club, we are not going to run for party leadership within the Democratic Party; we are going to run, whether the reformers run or not. We have another problem which determines that: We want to put reform Democrats who are radicals programmatically on the spot. We want to tell them: You run in the Democratic Party because you thought that the Democratic Party, and its reform movement, which is a liberal coalition, was the only place where you could function.

We will not invite into our political association activists who do not agree with our program. Here is a place where you can get active, here is a place where you fight out your program, not within an internal, narrow, sectarian group of Reform Democrats, where you lose every time, but within your own political association. If we can, we hope that we will utilize this educational forum to talk to radicals within the reform movement to pull them out, or at least to exercise them in their own consciousness about what they are doing. The process by which people are moved is not in terms of setting up, in an abstract sense, a political campaign or a political party, but in terms of the real struggles that people have participated in.

Now most of the people in our organization, just to answer your question, were people who came out of the movement, some of whom came out of the Reform Democrats. We were able to win them not because we promised the Democratic Party as an arena, because we didn't say that was the main thing, but we were able to win them because we said, we don't call you names because you happen to be in the Reform Democrats. We think that you are organizing for your ideological enemies. What you really have to do is organize into your own independent political movement.

If the Democratic Party becomes closed as an arena, even if it doesn't become closed, we consider independent politics as a real and a viable alternative, and we will engage in them wherever possible, wherever necessary. We don't think in the tactical sense that this should be an impediment to participating in the Democratic primary.

BARNES: This discussion is getting somewhere now. I just happen to have with me the program of this group that Stanley Aronowitz is a member of. It was passed out on the march on Washington. Not a program, OK, but a statement, a draft statement.

The difference between us here is that what one person sees as a tactic the other person sees as a principle. What one person sees as simply an arena of information the other person sees as the bedrock dividing line between the mode and character of educating and organizing for socialism in this country, or for any progressive social change. The concept that the Democratic Party is open now, and that it wasn't open at one time, may not be open in the future, is not the point. If you naturalize him, you could run Kosygin in some Democratic Party primaries in this country. And it wouldn't change the character of the Democratic primary.

The problem facing American society, the problem of American politics—let's look at the basic problem—is not organizing more people into the trade unions, it is not organizing more people into the civil rights movement, it is not getting a few more involved in protest against the war in Vietnam, although these are all important, especially the last one, because of the political character of the protest. The key question before American society is: Will the working class and the Negroes be capable of finding a way of independently organizing themselves politically? That class question is the key question; everything else revolves around that. Because it is only through an answer to that question that the next giant step forward can be taken. Everything else is not a sterile narrowing of possibilities or forms but the destruction and absorption of whatever radicalism exists into the channels of the Democratic Party, into the channels of the reform movement.

This Committee for Independent Political Action is a new thing and it's evolving. But there were ten signers on this statement. I heard one of them two Sundays ago explain his concept of what this is. A man named Henry Abrams stood up and explained that the reform movement in New York City is finished. It's incorrect to call the Committee for Independent Political Action a political party. That is not what it intends to be. What it intends to do is to go into the Democratic Party and replace the now sterile reform movement, in which it is impossible any longer to function, and to build a new reform Democratic wing.

ARONOWITZ: That's not the position.

BARNES: There are a lot of other people here who heard him. I only wanted to point out that so far four different signers of this Committee for Independent Political Action have been heard from as individuals and we've got four different views on the character of the Committee for Independent Political Action and four different views on the character of the Democratic Party and what it's like to work in it.

So the first thing to be said is, I'm not sure if anyone connected with this committee is sure exactly what their position is on this. However, let's look at the document itself a little further. It has a bunch of things which can be accepted by liberals, by radicals, even by Marxists, et cetera, as any broad thing would. They want to do canvassing, community organizing work on housing and schools. They want to participate in direct action, they want to engage in educational work, discussions, and forums. They want to build an independent radical constituency, they want to implement a program which specifically interrelates all the various issues we talked about earlier. And they want to create a political forum that can serve other communities and cities throughout the country.

Those are six of the seven basic points. So far it has absolutely zero programmatic content. In other words, for different political ends and for different purposes and for different individuals and classes one can do all of these things. I am not, I repeat, accusing or suggesting this is another version of the American Labor Party or anything else. I merely point out that these things are void of programmatic content. Lenin, Debs, and William Buckley can conduct community organizing, they can participate in organized actions, they can engage in educational work such as public discussions, forums, and the development of literature. They can participate in the development and organization of an independent radical constituency, they can attempt to interrelate civil rights, unemployment, poverty, education, and peace, and they can try to turn or use the form they create for this into a national model.

The only point that has any real programmatic content to it is this: They want to "lay the basis," in doing these things, "for an electoral campaign within the nineteenth congressional district in 1966." Fine. To me and the Socialist Workers Party, whether or not you run an election campaign is a tactical question. But then the big sentence comes: "We are prepared to run candidates in the Democratic primaries, or as independents." That's the only clue I have from reading this. Whether it's an attempt to go into a new Democratic reform movement, whether people will change their minds and see this as merely a way of getting into the Democratic reform movement and reject that and be given an independent candidate. If they do that, then the simple question that will arise is, under what program and for what reason and with what perspective are you going to do the other things?

I'm sure that the Socialist Workers Party and the Young Socialist Alliance and probably a lot of other forces on the left would very much like to enter into a discussion with the comrades who are involved in the Committee for Independent Political Action, as we will with anyone who raises these questions. The only other thing that I know about this is a statement that was passed out two weeks ago by the Committee for Independent Political Action, a draft statement in which they have a couple of pages saying essentially what we heard from the other speaker, about the character of American society, et cetera.

Then it goes on a little further. As I understand what you said, what you want to do in the Committee for Independent Political Action is to build a constituency around a program. Is that correct? Yes. That we are in complete agreement with, that is a giant step forward when any political group wants to do that. But the statement still leaves the thing up in the air, because it says that you do not reject the concept of coalition politics, that is, the basic concept of working in the Democratic Party, but you feel that this concept of whether you are coalitionists or not is secondary to the building of a radical constituency.

That seems to me the opposite of what was said, but it's in plain English. It goes on and explains once again: "We are prepared to run candidates in the Democratic primaries" and "we consider the question of the electoral forum to be tactical and secondary to the process of building a stable constituency."

What that does is bring you right back to the same question. Is anyone here against a stable constituency? Like is anyone against peace and independent politics? Everyone is for a stable constituency, everyone is for building the largest constituency possible, but the question is: On what political program and with what perspectives? What that means is back into the Democratic Party in one form or another or out of it to educate and recruit and bring young people to the concept of building a socialist party, leaving the character and program alone for a moment.

That is the basic dividing line. I find also disagreement among the people who are engaged in this project, which is fine. I just noticed the *Studies on the Left* editorial note that appeared two issues ago. I don't know if it was the majority of the editorial board or what, it appeared just as an editorial note. It points out that the fatal flaw of the Mississippi Freedom Democratic Party is its attempt to integrate itself into the Democratic Party. It explains very clearly how the role of the labor bureaucrats and civil rights leaders, and their reputations for New Deal liberalism, make it very easy for them to capture things like this. It ends up with this statement: "Atlantic City demonstrated that there is no room within the Democratic Party for insurgent local groups unwilling to compromise their constituents' demands for national party imperatives."

Well, there is either room or there is not. You can begin that way or you can't. What I would say as a minimum is that if you are going to build a new movement or a new party or a new organization you have to start out by stating clearly what you are for or what you are not for. You recruit on that or you recruit on whatever your program happens to be. If your activity is Democratic Party activity, you are building a radical constituency all right, but you are building radical Reform Democrats, whether you are personally opposed to it or not. That's the problem you face in organizing something like this.

ARONOWITZ: I would like to correct a couple of ideas that you have about it. We deliberately proceeded on the basis that we had to have a real ideological basis for activists to come in. Not civil rights, not peace, not minimum issues, but we had to have a statement. When you sign "I'm interested in joining CIPA" here, you get back this statement which, I think, pretty much explains where we are at.

It begins: "Most Americans have been cut off and excluded from the process of making the basic decisions that affect their lives. Partisan politics in the United States operates to sustain and extend the immediate and long-range interests of a relative handful of giant corporations and their institutional supporters, but the material and strategic interests and commitments of these corporations and their leaders, and the social values that flow from these interests, differ essentially from those of the poor, the workers, and most middle class Americans. In the determination of both domestic and foreign policy concern with the protection and extension of private property and profits takes priority over the personal and social needs of ordinary people. Domination of American politics by giant corporations has brought the United States to international crisis and to the organization of our lives around the ideological, political and material necessities of the cold war."

That's what we mean by independent politics. What we mean is that the political questions that we raise are not the kind of questions that could ever be raised in the reform movement of the Democratic Party or within the Johnson wing of the Democratic Party, by Buckley, by Bayard Rustin, or others, because we have made a political judgment about American politics which relates to the whole question of who controls.

Now the reason we regard the whole question of the Democratic Party, in New York City—not in Minnesota, Wisconsin, or any other place necessarily—as a tactical question is because of the history of political struggles in New York City. The reform movement of the Democratic Party is not an arena in which we can really develop a radical politics. And so we cut people off from that. There were many people who were involved in the California Democratic clubs who learned a lesson out of their experience—real sensuous, concrete experiences. And so they went into organizations like the VDC [Vietnam Day Committee]. And we built a radicalism. Tom Hayden, Todd Gitlin, Paul Potter, Paul Booth—every last one of the organizers of SDS, which is the real key organization of the antiwar movement, began in liberal study groups of the National Student Association.

The real problem is not whether Tom and the other people in SDS have rejected or accepted the Democratic Party as an arena of political action. We know they are radicals. And the reason we know they are radicals is because SDS organized the best goddamned march on the Vietnam issue, which is the crux of the whole question of politics in this country today, and nobody else organized it. And what made them organize it was the fact that they had gone through a process of political experience. Not a process of liberalism reinforced by liberalism, which is the old SP-CP pattern. Not that kind of situation, but where they began to recognize where control was.

When Paul Potter got up at the SDS march and said it is the corporations that are the enemy, and we have to name the enemy in this country, that was the most important, primary precondition for politics, that was the content, that was the principle, that was the dividing line. The dividing line is not where you choose your forum—the Democratic Party is a temporary, transient kind of tactical situation because it is a place which has permitted participation of different positions.

The Democratic Party primary says that we have to get 350 signatures in an assembly district and 1,500 signatures in a congressional district to get on the ballot. It does not tell us what to say, how to say it, or how to mobilize. And it's not really the center of our movement. The center of our movement is to organize and educate around this concept. But not to organize and educate depending upon the TV and the radio and the press to give us publicity. Instead, to educate on the basis of canvassing, house-by-house canvassing and community organizing around the rent strikes.

How many radicals who have good programs have been involved in the rent strikes? I have. I have been with eighteen tenants at different times down to Mayor Wagner's office, and all we were able to do was to get rid of Mayor Wagner, by our activity of the boycott and the sit-ins in the rent strikes.

We have never been able to develop any kind of political position that has been meaningful to tenants, that has been meaningful to workers. Now I think that the problem is how you find those forums to talk to people, not to talk to them in the way of finding the minimum common denominator, that's not the problem, but to find the forums where you will be listened to, where you will have a forum, and if that forum happens to be within the Democratic primary—and not in the Democratic Party because the Democratic Party means you run in a party election, we are not going to run in any party elections—this primary gives us one forum. Then we go on and we run in November independently.

By the way, Governor Rockefeller has given us a way of doing this beautifully. He says that we are now going to have a Democratic primary in June and a general election in November. That means that if we run in June we have one chance of getting before people a program, an educational program. We ain't going to win, don't kid yourself, and we are not going to invite reformers into the political movement either. But then we can go ahead and get our independent petitions for the general election signed. And this is not an unusual practice.

The point is that we are ready to discuss what tactic is proper at any one time. And if we determine as a result of a serious discussion that we should not go into the Democratic primary, we will not go into the Democratic primary, because we are not wedded to the coalition concept. And when we say in this statement that coalitions are secondary, we don't mean the coalition question as raised by Rustin, we mean coalitions with the Socialist Workers Party and coalitions with the Communist Party—that is a secondary question to our common need to go out and build a radical constituency, a radical base for a program.

I'm prepared to vote for any radical socialist candidate that runs for office. And I think that those candidates should be run. What I'm trying to do is not to develop radical politics on the old bases which divide the left. I'm for a coalition of the left. A coalition which is based on a program. And if we can discuss the question of tactics we will discuss the question of tactics. But if you get hung up on the question of whether you are in the Democratic primary, and not the Democratic Party, then I think you effectively exclude yourself from the opportunity of developing a radical program that has any meaning.

QUESTION: This is a brief question to Mr. Aronowitz, which can be answered briefly. While you are telling people what the ruling class's role is and all of the things that they are against, and while you are running a candidate in the nineteenth congressional district, who do you tell them to vote for in the main elections?

ARONOWITZ: We are not Democrats asking people to support the Democratic ticket. We are not going to enter into a coalition with Mayor Wagner or with Abraham Beame. We would not enter into a coalition with [Congressman William F.] Ryan unless we saw that he was prepared to accept our position. We are not looking for that kind of electoral coalition. What we hope to have happen, very frankly, is not that this community organizing thing will be confined to this.

What we expect, or we hope, is that other people will take it up. Look at the seventh congressional district in Berkeley, where Jeffrey Cohelan is the best liberal Democrat that you can find, outside of a guy like Phil Burton, if you take issues. I understand that the antiwar movement is preparing to run against Phil Burton. Well, that has been the direct inspiration of the kind of movement that we've started here. What we hope to emerge is a confluence of a lot of local movements that experiment, that don't have any real solid answers.

I wish I had this surety that Jack Barnes has and that some people have about where the direction is. We have to experiment, we have to grope. The only thing we have is our ideology. With that, there is no compromise. Maybe it's a difference in experience. But we're clear, I think it's fairly clear what we mean. We mean that if you accept the view that the priorities of this country are developed out of the cold war context, that we have to end that context, by ending neocolonialism and American imperialism, then you belong in this movement. Therefore we are not reform, because reform believes that you work in coalitions around electoral alliances that do not understand the central question.

Now there is another difference. And I'll just make that very brief. The difference is the old concept of the united front that was developed by the CP and the SP in the thirties and a new concept of what a united front could be now. In this country the application by a number of radicals of the idea of united action was that we organize for Roosevelt, and Jack did a brilliant job on that. I think that the only way we can prevent thousands of students and thousands of other people from falling back into the trap of organizing for lesser evils is if we develop a political alternative that is meaningful to them. And we think that this kind of thing can be meaningful to them, not because of the primary, but because most of our concepts arise out of experience.

QUESTION: Mr. Aronowitz, in the Democratic primaries only registered Democrats can vote. In the Republican primaries only registered Republicans vote. I understand that you are going to go into the primary in order to convince the registered Democrats that you are against the Democrats.
ARONOWITZ: That's right.

QUESTION: Do you exclude going into the Republican primaries to convince the Republicans that you are against the Republicans? And do you think this is an effective way of boring from within these parties to organize an independent party?
ARONOWITZ: Well, we're back to the old saw. We are not going into the Democratic Party, we are going into the Democratic primary. You don't see the difference, but there is a difference, and the difference is evident to anybody who knows about the operations of the Democratic Party.

For one thing the situation in New York City is the following, and we've done a little study. More than 90 percent of Negroes and Puerto Ricans and workers happen to be registered Democrats or registered Liberals; there is only 10 percent of that group in the population that happens to be registered Republican, and that's one factor. We are not looking at what party we are going into, we are looking at where the constituency is.

The second thing is, that the real vote that takes place, and the way in which politics operates in this city is that the big battles, what most people worry about, in terms of where the politics is, have been within the Democratic primary in the nineteenth congressional district. I know the nineteenth congressional district; in this district, the Republican gets 28 percent or 29 or sometimes 30 percent of the vote. Therefore, where the people vote significantly, where they make choices, is not in the general election. They tend to make choices in the Democratic primary. That's where the action is, that's where all the pressure and all of the activity and all of the debate takes place, in the nineteenth congressional district.

What we are going to say, if we go into that primary, not that party, is that neither of these men has anything to say about the problems of the people of this district that is different from what the administration has been promulgating. What we are going to say is that our needs in this district can only be met if we accept a whole different idea.

The point is that we expect that when other movements around the country develop a serious national political movement, the whole idea of going into the Democratic primary will become unnecessary, because then we'll have a national program and a national movement that is able to project a real national struggle. We are not in that position now. We are in a position of starting locally because we think that it is not possible to do it on a mass basis nationally.

QUESTION: I'm just wondering about a very practical problem. One, I assume that if you're serious, you are urging people to register to vote. Now having participated in politics here in New York City we are aware of the fact that anyone who votes in the primary is ineligible to sign a nominating petition to put independent candidates on the ballot in the general election. Now whatever your intention, it means that you would have to urge people to register and vote in the Democratic primary.

If you should happen to win in that district—and that's not inconceivable—your candidate will be what? He will be the candidate of the Democratic Party machine. That's the whole point of participating in politics, that is, in the Democratic Party primary.

ARONOWITZ: You made a very valid point. That's something that we are going to have to consider, and again you raise a practical question.

If it is true that people cannot then sign petitions the second time if they signed the first petition, and since we need 6,000 signatures in order to get 1,500 good ones, that might be a practical consideration.

As to the second part of your question, we don't have any serious illusions about winning. That's not the name of the game. You come into this politics with that kind of position, and you're going to find yourself really very quickly being attacked by everybody and being operated on in all sorts of ways that are not going to permit you to win. Especially if you are true and honest to your program, which is, by the way, the reason we developed the draft statement before we permitted anybody to join the association in its organizing phase....

Now one thing I would like to appeal. I've given as many answers as I'm going to give on the issue of the party primary versus the Democratic Party. This is not in our judgment the key to independent political action. In our judgment that is something that we can debate down the road. The key question is whether you are willing to go out into the neighborhood and organize on the issues, and organize people for politics.

The radical movement has in the past been afraid to go out into communities and organize people on independent political positions because it is much easier to work in coalitions on the one hand, and it's much easier to be pure on the other. It is much easier to have your full program, your full position, your guy who really agrees with you in your own particular version, and so on. What we think is important in this country is not how you come to an antiwar, anti-Johnson position, but that you are there....

QUESTION: There was one point raised, and that is the question of the antiwar movement. I want both speakers to comment on this. Stanley said that in his opinion any movement like the antiwar movement couldn't be successful, couldn't explain its goals and aims, and expressed a certain pessimism about the antiwar movement as such. I want both speakers to comment on whether they think that the antiwar movement in itself can bring about a change in American foreign policy and an end to the war.

ARONOWITZ: I think that that is a very good question. Liberals have the illusion that given the present state of American politics, a pressure movement against the Vietnam War, unless it had a real base among Negroes, Puerto Ricans, and workers, unless we had a real working class base in the antiwar movement, that we could change the policy either by the brilliance of our intellect or by the sharp cutting edge of our protest.

I think our immediate task is out of the antiwar movement to build a political movement that sees things in terms that I've discussed. I don't think that we should place ourselves in the position that SANE did around the bomb-testing thing—beginning to work out tactical questions as to how you get the best kind of nuclear test ban treaty. Our problem is to see what kind of connection we can make between war and the system of rule, number one, and what kind of connections we can make between war and people's needs in the communities.

I think that the antiwar movement will effect changes only if it acts with its most militant, its sharpest kind of acts. That when it begins to think, as many politicians do, about winning, when it begins to think about the problems of how we influence the government's policy in tactical terms, this was all I was talking about, then it really gets into trouble.

The reason I come to this is because I have, for better or worse, a lot of contact with people who are in the movement. I spoke in Berkeley about a lot of the same things I'm talking about today. And there were people burnt out, they were no longer interested in the movement. I talked to SNCC people in New York, who had been in SNCC in Mississippi, and they are no longer really in the movement, they are discouraged because they lack a perspective about the possibilities of victory, about what the real objectives of the movement were for themselves. As activists, they really believed that when they went through this public demonstration of activity, that that was going to result in significant changes in government policy, because they accepted the essential notion of democratic pluralism that I described before: that pressure really does work. What they found was that, faced with this tremendous power of our opponent and the intractability of his policy, they saw no hope within the framework of pressure to win, either now or any time in the future.

What I'm saying is that the antiwar movement is a training ground for people to come to the perspective of opposition. You might even want to call it socialism. This is the only place you can go. Now the movement itself, as a single-issue movement, is limited unless it is able to establish connections with workers and Negro people, and it won't do that if it maintains the moral tone of an antiwar protest, even if it makes a political criticism of the war itself.

It will make those connections only if it is able to tie up the interests of workers and Negro people and what they are being deprived of as a result of the war. When that happens, then we have a chance to think about a mass antiwar movement that can change the policy, that will in effect be political, and then I will come back to this microphone and say that the next step we have is winning. That is, changing the policy. But we are not in that position now. So we have to see the objectives of the movement in different terms. And that's the only thing I meant by that.

BARNES: . . . I think the tendency still among radicals, even in the antiwar movement itself, is to underestimate its importance, impact, and meaning. I'll go out on a limb. I don't think it's excluded that the antiwar movement and its development along the lines it is traveling now could be a major factor in stopping the war in Vietnam. I think that's a real possibility, and should be fought for.

The important thing about the antiwar movement is its growth and development to embrace thousands and thousands of people in this country in the middle of a war. What it represents is something unique, that is, a degree and layer of radicalization to Johnson's policy, in direct opposition to Johnson and the Democratic administration, that was completely unexpected.

The best possible thing that can be done is to continue to build and organize this movement around the two basic axes it was started on in the march on Washington, that is, the exclusion of no individual with regard to his membership or nonmembership in any other organization, and the concrete mobilizations around the demand to take the troops out of Vietnam. There is no limit to the number of people in American society that that idea can be attractive to and can be picked up by.

In fact, the only antiwar movements that have ever been successful in history as far as stopping a war have been those movements where the troops themselves, and those who influence the troops, and those who can be the troops, demand that they come home, that they stop fighting. So from this point of view the best possible thing to do is to continue to build the antiwar movement.

It is important to separate this from the second question that was raised, because they are two separate questions. That is, the antiwar movement as a growing movement based on the idea of bringing the troops home has just begun to penetrate the tens and hundreds of thousands of people in this country who can be mobilized around that basic single idea regardless of all other differences they have. The second is the development of a program for social change, of joining or forming a socialist organization.

There is no contradiction between the two. Those who have a program and an idea and a concept of building a socialist party or a socialist movement or an organization, I'm sure, will spend much of their time, when they are in contact with the people in this antiwar movement, trying to convince them of this and involving them in it. But this does not contradict in any way the building and developing of this antiwar movement.

If there is anything in this country that threatens to break up old alliances, raise questions, and radicalize people, it is this antiwar movement. There are people that this movement has forced to think, outside the student milieu. GIs, workers, Negroes, middle class people, anyone you want to name—they have all felt the impact of this movement more than they have felt the impact of anything else in recent times. Because it cuts right through the pretensions of coalescing around Johnson and accepting at face value his program. The direction it has is total opposition to Johnson. The only thing that can harm it is to try to channel it away from this in some other form.

QUESTION: Stanley Aronowitz holds up the Debs Socialist Party as an example to emulate in becoming a mass radical party. What puzzles me about your position is this inconsistency. The Socialist Party was converted into a mass party on two bases: One, it rejected any connection whatsoever with the Democratic Party; on the other side, it came out forthrightly as a socialist, anticapitalist party, proclaiming that message at all times, electoral and otherwise. As I listened to you, you stated that it is quite possible to have certain types of connections with the Democratic Party; on the other hand, you and others, as you are organizing, will not come out forthrightly as socialists. Now, why is it that if the Socialist Party is the model to follow, you do not propose following it in the decisive respects in which it did become a mass party?

This very discussion on these two issues was held up and down this avenue and in this district from 1900 to 1912, maybe in this very hall or in this building, thousands of times. The right wing, those who resisted and rejected building a Socialist Party in New York City, in this district and in others, said, "No, we can't cut ourselves off from the Democratic Party, we can't come out directly as socialists," for the precise reasons you gave; but they were not the ones who actually built the Debs Socialist Party.

ARONOWITZ: I think that that is a very challenging question, it was very well put. The only difference between 1900 and 1920, I talked about the form of the Socialist Party and its conscious attempt to become a mass party. We've had a difference, a fundamental difference in the development and the history of American capitalism that has been richly described in a number of places, including Art Preis's book.

The difference is essentially this. We've had the emergence of state capitalism, not only in the management of the economy and the development of a permanent cold war economy which has had the effect of giving us relatively full employment for a large segment of American workers. But we've also had the emergence of a welfare system which has enlarged the system of domination of the corporations in a new way. Not only in the old coercive sense in which Marx and Lenin talked about the role of the state, but in a new way of coercion that is related to welfare. And what has happened is that, because of the fact that the United States has emerged as the dominant capitalist country of the world and has been able to stabilize its economic functioning, relatively speaking, since 1940, consciousness has changed.

The second major development has been the assimilation of large numbers of people into the country and the loosening of the old socialist ties that were developed in Eastern Europe, in Germany, and in other parts of the world, which means that ethnic assimilation, to a large extent, has also become political and ideological assimilation, which I deplore.

The third thing that's become clear to me is that consciousness has changed with respect to the whole idea of socialism, because socialism in this country has been distorted by, number one, the development of the welfare system, which is not socialism, but which gives people a new understanding and usually a negative understanding of the state as well as a positive understanding of taking care of personal welfare; and the emergence of the Soviet Union, China, and other countries, which become the picture of socialism for people in this country.

I don't believe that we can develop a picture of socialism similar to that of the Socialists in 1912 when we have already had a history of forty-five years of world socialism, of some kind or another, and still blithely go along and talk about socialism as though it never existed.

I'm for socialism. And I'm for a party of socialism. I am, however, for discussing socialism in American contexts. Not to change the basic problem of ownership of the means of production or the basic problem of the control of the machinery of politics and of life. That's not the problem. The problem is to be able to translate and develop new concepts of what socialism means in the light of the welfare system, in the light of the fact that we do have a Soviet Union and a China.

The other thing which is also important is that the purveyor of welfare in this country was not the working class movement alone. There have been some mistakes made in the writing of history. We think of ourselves, that is, the working class and socialist movements, as being the ones who carried the program and gave it and forced it through our mass action. Now, I think that's true. And that tells part of the story, just like the ending of the war in Vietnam will have been partly the result of the protest that we have now developed.

I think, however, if you look into the history of organizations like the National Civic Federation, an organization of 5,000 members, including people in the largest corporations, including Gerard Swope of GE, you will find that the concept of welfarism, and the concept of laborism against socialism, was developed as early as 1913, 1914, 1916, and 1920.

So we do have in this country a peculiar brand, similar to what Bismarck initiated in Germany, of corporate-sponsored liberal welfare capitalism. It changes the nature of the problems that we have to confront in a new socialist movement.

What we have to do now is pick at and develop opposition to what are essentially the weakest and most vulnerable parts of our system, which are, number one, the fact that war is not a policy, but a function of this system. We are always talking about war as a policy, that we are going to stop the war in Vietnam by our mass action. Until we have done that we may stop Vietnam but we are not going to stop the Dominican Republic and the whole situation in Latin America. And, number two, we have to make the connection between the fight for democracy, that is, the fight for control, and the operations of the welfare system, because that is what is most relevant in people's lives. . . .

I regret the emergence of ideological socialist movements in the 1920s based on the developments in world socialism. Not because I don't think that we in this country had to be at any time favorable and friendly to any revolution, because the Socialist Party was, up until 1923, favorable to the Bolshevik revolution, the Hungarian revolution. What happened in this country was that we began to develop as part of a world movement a consciousness of American socialism that was dependent upon that world movement, and I say we have to move away from that. We cannot be basically for the National Liberation Front as a slogan for the peace movement in this country. We have to be against

U.S. involvement, we have to be for withdrawal, we have to express sympathy with revolutions and not participate as if we were Vietnamese peasants.

We are American people with all kinds of different consciousness and different problems. And so what I think is that we have really, in a sense, to develop a new, a more real concept of American socialism and American independent political action that corresponds to all the changes that have taken place in the capitalist system. The leopard has not changed its character, but to a certain extent it has changed its spots.

SUMMARIES

ARONOWITZ: . . . The thing that separates Barnes and me in my judgment is not the kind of thing that separates us from Rustin and Harrington. I think the lessons of the sixties, of the last five years, and the lessons of the thirties, are that we have to build a mass movement on our own program. That really is what counts, because in the long run our relevance to the process by which American politics is controlled and relates to the economy and to the whole society is where the masses are in motion around the socialist program we all want. If we can't find the way to do that we are condemned into ways and means of picking at the liberal establishment and its institutions and trying to win individual converts to our positions.

What we really have to get away from is the whole psychology, which is really based on your profound pessimism rather than my pessimism about the war and our ability to change it. We have to get away from the psychology that Americans are essentially conservative and liberal in content. I think that that is becoming less and less true, and my experience in the labor movement is convincing me that it is only the leadership that prevents the workers from moving in better directions because we don't have—I'll use an old Leninist term—we don't have the cadre to be able to crystallize the frustrations that exist on an elementary level in the shops and are insoluble on the shop level, that are insoluble within the framework of the old ideological reliance on the cold war.

Workers can understand that, once the alternatives are presented. We just don't have the people who are able to present it. The problem is to find meaningful ways of developing a program that is radical and that challenges the question of power, and then we have to go out and try to do it in communities, shops, and other institutions of our society.

BARNES: Stanley Aronowitz said that one of the reasons they were charting the path they were in the Committee for Independent Political Action is that they don't want to pose things in the old ways which divided the left. Maybe this is where one of our differences is.

Let me just end up by saying what I think divides the left in the United States. What divides the American left, what the lines of division are between our party—the Socialist Workers Party—and the Communist and Socialist parties, is the question of independent politics versus coalitionism, the question of a revolutionary perspective to change American society and to take power out of the hands of the capitalists; or a basically reformist perspective, whether it is hidden in the guise of radical phraseology and maneuverism or it is open and clear-cut, class struggle versus class collaboration.

We've had a combination of both these for the past thirty years in this country. The key is not arguing over whether Paul Booth and Paul Potter and Stanley Aronowitz and Clark Kissinger and everyone else are radicals or not. Whether or not they are radicals is not defined by the march on Washington, by rent strikes, by anything like that. No. They are also not defined by which of them goes into politics. The question is what kind of politics and for what reason.

It was not wrong, it was not an error for the working class radicals in the thirties to organize for John L. Lewis, as it was put earlier. The problem was the incapacity of the majority of them to understand and project an independent political path parallel to the economic path that would have made the CIO movement politically independent of the ruling class parties. It was this basic lack and this basic problem which faces us today and which determined, more than any other single factor, the decline and stagnation of the American labor movement. So the problem was not directly the corporations, the changes in the corporations, the change in the character of imperialism. Nor is it the ability to grant reforms and concessions—an ability that is not going to last nearly as long as some may think. It is essentially the state power based on the instruments of control, the political instruments, the Republican and Democratic parties, which are used to maintain this power.

Only the perspective of convincing the workers and Negroes to turn away from this and organizing them around a program which projects a revolutionary socialist change of American society will solve the problem.

Should progressives work in the Democratic Party?

Carl Haessler vs. George Breitman

The following debate took place on May 8, 1959, at Eugene V. Debs Hall in Detroit, Michigan. It was the last year of conservative Republican Dwight D. Eisenhower's second term in the White House, when the Democrats controlled both houses of Congress and the state government in Michigan.

It was also the end of a decade that had brought about the decimation of the whole radical movement, thanks to the Korean War and the witch hunts unleashed by McCarthy, Truman, and the union bureaucracy. Relative economic prosperity, although marred by intermittent recessions, contributed to the conservative climate. International events—the end of the Stalin cult in the Soviet Union; workers' rebellions in East Germany, Poland, and Hungary; and the spread of colonial revolution in Asia and the Caribbean—encouraged a regroupment in the badly battered American Left; in 1958 this had led several radical groups and individuals, including the Socialist Workers Party, to launch a United Independent-Socialist ticket in the New York election of governor and U.S. senator.

The debate was an exploration of the possibility of radical regroupment in Michigan, where the labor movement of the period was headed by Walter Reuther of the United Auto Workers, James Hoffa of the International Brotherhood of Teamsters, and August Scholle, president of the Michigan AFL-CIO.

This debate was originally published as a pamphlet by the Friday Night Socialist Forum.

Should progressives work in the Democratic Party?

PRESENTATIONS

CARL HAESSLER: I wonder why I was asked to participate in this debate. Knowing the gang that the first speaker, the affirmative speaker, would be up against, I suppose the manager of the forum decided it would take a brave man to come up here and present that point of view. I tried it about a year ago at the Central Methodist Church, where I was the unaffiliated speaker, and three other third-party speakers had the floor, and I got a pretty good drubbing, but it didn't bother me, especially as one middle-aged bourgeois member of the audience came up and said, "I thank you very much. You have the same persuasive character of presenting the subject as Dr. Henry Hitt Crane." And I don't know if he thought that was complimentary or not, but I have been compared to preachers before this, although that is not exactly my line.

However, I am serious in taking this side of the case, and

not from inexperience. Almost fifty years ago, I debated on this general subject, except it was capitalist parties vs. Socialist Party, at the University of Wisconsin. One of my opponents, white-haired like myself, took one of the opposing views, and I imagine he'll take the floor in the general discussion tonight. I was a Socialist Party member, very active in Milwaukee after I was fired from the University of Illinois. I reached the glory of being a member of the City Central Committee of the Socialist Party there, and also of the five-man State Executive Committee of the Socialist Party. Later on I was active in campaigning for Senator La Follette when he ran for President in 1924, which was supposed to be the extension to the country as a whole of the third party—the Progressive Party—that had been founded in the state of Wisconsin. And when Henry Wallace, an ex-Republican, ran for President in 1948, also using the name of the Progressive Party, I was somewhat active in that campaign. In fact, I remember a debate here in which a lawyer for the Republican Party, a professor for the Democratic Party, and yours truly for the Progressive Party discussed the platforms. Well, let's get down to the subject, "Should Progressives Work in the Democratic Party?"

I take that to mean, should progressives, who are interested in organized political action, work in the Democratic Party? If you are a progressive along general, vague social lines, and don't spend much time on political parties, I would say, don't work in any political party. Why work in a party if you're not politically, organizationally interested? So I wonder if my adversary will accept that restriction of the subject. I hope he does, because he has plenty of ammunition besides that, because a year ago, the Democratic Party was much cleaner-looking than it is today. Since the November victory, the sweeping November victory of the Democrats in the national election, great things were expected of that party by the labor people who supported it, supported them with money, with speeches, and most of all, with work in the precincts. So far, there has not been very much visible fruit on the national scale, for labor or for progressives, of this victory of the Democratic Party.

In the state of Michigan, of course, there has been some fruit. I should say, for instance, the victory of the Democratic Party in the last elections, not only in '58, but in '56, '54, '50, '48—that those victories have paved the way, for instance, for the Democratic control of the state supreme court for the first time in the history of that body. Democrats were tied once before with the Republicans, but this is the first time that the Democrats have a 5-3 edge in the state supreme court. And it was due solely to the fact that Governor Williams, elected by original Democrats and by labor Democrats over and over again, had the opportunity to fill vacancies by appointment on the supreme court, and those appointees, in almost all cases, except for Justice Clark Adams, were elected when the time came for them to face the voters. And as you know, the greatest fruit of the state supreme court Democratic control was the decision in the Ford strike unemployment benefit case. They reversed the previous Republican decision that strikers in one plant of the Ford company would make all members thrown out of work—all employees thrown out of work at the Ford Motor Company—ineligible for unemployment benefits. The Republicans, representing General Motors and Ford, thought this was sound doctrine. The Democrats this year, representing labor and Democrats generally, thought the other interpretation was sound. Well, that's the most outstanding supreme court labor victory that has been achieved, I think, anywhere in the United States. And it has been achieved in a state where labor—organized labor—has for all practical purposes captured the Democratic Party.

The Democratic Party, without labor, in this state had been nothing except a governor once in a while who couldn't get anywhere with a Republican legislature. Now with the appointive power in Democratic hands for the courts for these many years—for the circuit courts, the probate courts, the common pleas courts—here and throughout the state, the judicial temper of a corporation-minded reactionary court in an industrial state has been decisively altered, and I ask you whether this could have been done by any other political means than the means that were actually employed. For instance, to make it personal, because that's what brings it down to cases, could the Socialist Workers Party, with its 4,000 votes in the spring election in the state of Michigan, have done anything even approaching that? Could the Socialist Labor Party, with a few thousand more votes throughout the state, have done anything in that line? I don't have to ask you if the Republican Party could have done it. They could have, but they wouldn't have. The Democratic Party got in a position to do something on the supreme court and they did it.

Of course one of the justices on the supreme court is a socialist, a man who spent thirty days in jail in the good old militant days of '37, for defying a Republican judge's anti-labor injunction—Justice George Edwards of the supreme court; and of course the state chairman of the Democratic Party several times ran for office as a socialist, in and around Ann Arbor; and the man who controls the money bags of the Democratic Party, Walter Reuther, was a socialist within my own experience. In fact in 1938, when I was functioning to some degree as his brain truster—I founded his local union paper and edited it for a number of years—Reuther consulted me as to whether he should continue paying dues to the Socialist Party. I said no. And we discussed it, and I said if you want to rise in the UAW and reach an important position, and if you'll then want to spread your activities beyond that, don't get tangled up with a small group that's getting nowhere, even faster than Norman Thomas is growing older, but get out from under. Don't have these entangling little alliances sticking to you. Free yourself. And he did. And he freed himself to such a great degree that a few weeks ago, when Jimmy Hoffa, who used to be his friend in West Side strikes, accused Reuther of being a socialist, Reuther said he hadn't ever been in the Socialist Party except one year, during the depression. I know myself he had been a Socialist Party member for five years, and his father had been for thirty or forty years before that, but he's entitled to a change of opinion and he's entitled to change his memory of the facts too. If there are other people with better memories than he has, well, that's their hard luck, because he'll deny it, and everybody will believe him and nobody will believe those who have counterevidence.

Well, you see, with three former socialists at the controls of the Democratic Party in this state, things are beginning to be done. But you still have a die-hard Republican senate, as a result of that overbalanced legislature created by an amendment to the constitution, but even that will crumble. Some senators are fearing for their seats, some Republican senators; some of them, while they're not exactly afraid for their seats, are ready to make deals with the majority party in the senate and even more so in the House, and so I think Michigan is a very good example of progressives working for organized political action in the majority party, the Democratic Party of this state.

Now, there are similar achievements, not quite so great, in other states. There is the state of West Virginia. I was sitting in the United Mine Workers office in Washington, talking to Denny Lewis, the brother of John L., and he was criticizing Reuther, saying he was wasting a lot of money on labor political action, "and we don't go in for that." And I said, "No, you don't, except in West Virginia." And he said, "Right, Carl." In West Virginia, the United Mine Workers controls the Democratic Party, and they've elected two U.S.

senators, ousting the Republicans in the last election, and they control the governor, most of the legislature. West Virginia has very good mining legislation, and considering that it's a hillbilly state, up in the mountains, not much doing industrially, West Virginia has a pretty fair record, legislatively, as far as states go. That legislative record was established by the Democratic Party, which is owned by the United Mine Workers of America.

Now let's take the state of Minnesota, where the Democratic Party is so thoroughly controlled by the old Farmers Non-Partisan League, the radical farmers in the state, and by the unions, that it really isn't even called the Democratic Party. It's called the Farmer-Labor Democratic Party. And in Minnesota, they've done pretty well, too. They elected a senator, Eugene McCarthy, to supplant the old Republican diehard, Senator Thye; they've elected a good number of liberal congressmen, they've got a Democratic governor, and things in that state are coming along too. Of course, they've got judicial drags, and there are legislative drags; the press is not Democratic, to say nothing of being prolabor, but there's a state on the move too.

You take those three states—Michigan, Minnesota, and West Virginia—and you have a start for a pretty fair infiltration by progressive labor, meaning those people who are interested in organized political action, toward the beginning of a labor party under the Democratic name. Then if you consider that California went whole-hog against the Republicans in November, and the Democrats control not only all the state offices, except one, I believe, but both houses of the legislature, and that good legislation is going through, there's another state—a state, of course, of crackpots, especially around Los Angeles, but crackpots often make good organizers and good advance guards for the progressives in the party.

And then, north of California, the longshoremen, Bridges's union, the lumber men, and the building trades have had for many years a tight legislative conference which put the fear of labor, if not the fear of God, into the legislators; and lo and behold, in 1958, two of the remaining Republican congressmen—the state has four congressmen—were defeated; one Republican is left, three are now Democrats in Congress, and both Oregon senators are Democrats, where for years and years, no Democrat was ever sent East. The governor had been a Democrat. A liberal Republican defeated him this year, but the legislature keeps track of him, and Oregon is doing pretty well. The legislature, just a few weeks ago, adopted a resolution urging Eisenhower to relax the controls on trade with China. Of course, they did it for business reasons, but there you are, with one more state. North of Oregon is Washington, with a similar record, not quite so advanced, but getting there.

Then you take the state of New York in the East. Of course, the needle trades union sabotaged the promising third party movement when they split the American Labor Party to form a liberal wing. The American Labor Party has since become defunct; the Liberal Party has not yet been buried, but maybe it will revive, or maybe something else will take its place. The defeat of the Democrats in New York City, New York State, because the party there listened to the Tammany gangsters instead of organized labor, is something that will be remembered, and there's a much better chance than for any of the splinter parties, the little parties, to work.

Now I'd like to make it plain again that I'm not opposed to small parties, to small parties as such; they keep the torch burning and are the vanguard of political thinking, and political feeling, which is even more important than thinking. But they don't accomplish anything in this country in an organized political way. It's the major parties, one or the other, that should be infiltrated, and then captured. And the Democratic Party, which is falling apart in two sections—has been for a number of generations—is the most promising, and the results I've cited should encourage us to go on with that. The other Democratic states of an industrial character, where the unions are strong, like Connecticut with its big sweep of Congress in the '58 election; Massachusetts, where the Democrats finally got control of the state senate (they already had the lower house); and New Jersey, where a Republican was retired for a Democratic U.S. senator; and Ohio—I know Ohio is regarded by the *Militant* and other groups as a shining example of what happens when you use the Democratic Party instead of smaller parties for your work—but Ohio is just in the beginning of the Democratic capture, the Democratic infiltration by labor, and you'll see results there too.

Now what is the objection to this point of view? I've heard it before, and I'm not going to take away George's thunder by outlining it to you. All I want to say is that anything you can say against the Democratic Party you can say—and much more—against the Republican Party. I would like my opponent in this discussion to take up the points that I have presented, of considering the practicality of organized political action by taking over an already established party, instead of going through the agony of trying to set up one of your own.

The members of the Socialist Workers Party, who are very strong pluggers for third party action, who work day and night, especially in campaign time, tirelessly too through the rest of the year, certainly excite my admiration. If their purpose is to keep alive a certain doctrine, presented to any who'll listen, I will say that's fine. But if their purpose is to capture political control of the community, of the state, or of the nation, then I think they are taking the road that is long, tortuous, full of detours, obstacles, costly, and in the end, barring a revolution, unsuccessful. And why?

Well, I think the Socialist Workers Party members know

the difficulties, for instance, of merely getting on the ballot in industrial states. The fatigue, the disappointment, the cheating against petition circulators that those in control of political action exercise, if they fear they might lose some precinct or some ward or some district because a third party is in the picture. And then, also, the inability to attract followers, in that the American voter is swayed not by reason but by emotion, and the emotion of enjoying a defeat is not widespread enough to make a good third party feasible. There should be some prospect of winning once in a while, in order to attract the mass American voter. I don't see it in any of the third parties that have emerged so far.

I have one more point. The organization of a party, of a third party, is a terrific job, and a very disappointing job, and if you have a party shell already set up for you, why not take it over? It's a good Wall Street game, like the American Car and Foundry Company being taken over by lawyers and financiers, to become A.C.F. Wrigley's—Wrigley's Super Markets. The corporate setup is all there. And so with the Democrats, the political setup is all there. And if you think you can't sneak up and capture it, you have less imagination and power of adaptive action than I give you credit for. You've captured three key states—Minnesota, West Virginia, Michigan—then you capture another state, and then for a while there's a setback because the glowing prospects that were held out by the party speakers don't come true all at once. The takeover has to be postponed a little bit. There are obstacles, but at least you're on the right road. Now, George, you knock that down!

GEORGE BREITMAN: I shall begin defining what I have in mind by the terms "progressive," "work in," and "Democratic Party."

By "progressive" I mean two things: First, the great social forces that have the power to decide the future—the working class and its allies, the working farmers, the Negro people, and the youth. Second, I have in mind the smaller, radical groups and individuals who are repelled by the capitalist system, its anarchy, militarism, depressions, regimentation, inequality, and debasement of human and cultural values, and who favor the replacement of this system by one based on cooperation, planning, brotherhood, and promotion of the interests of the majority. In short, I use the term "progressive" for those who are prolabor or anticapitalist, who are antiwar, antifascist, and anti–Jim Crow, prosocialist.

By "work in" I mean belong to, become a member of, vote for, support, or endorse.

Now, about the nature of the Democratic Party. Socialists say that political parties represent, express, reflect class interests. This doesn't mean that parties necessarily *say* they represent class interests; nor that all their members think they do; nor even that all their members come from the same class. (The truth of this proposition doesn't depend on what socialists say, or what antisocialists say. It can be tested by facts, the evidence of history, objective analysis.)

When socialists say the Democratic Party is a capitalist party, they don't mean that most of its members are capitalists. Obviously not. If the capitalists had to depend on their own numbers, they couldn't elect a justice of the peace, for they are a tiny part of the population. Actually, most supporters of the Democratic Party are workers, farmers, and members of the middle classes. But they aren't the ones who decide the real aims of the party.

Nationally, the Democratic Party is a coalition—of capitalists and union leaders, of southern white supremacists and northern Negroes, of corrupt machines in the cities and unorganized or loosely organized farmers on the land, of conservatives and liberals, et cetera.

This coalition explains why the Democratic Party says the things it says, why it writes the platforms it writes—

for it appeals to conflicting interests and tries to hold them together. It also explains why the Democratic Party sometimes says different things than the other capitalist party, the Republican Party, for the Republican Party has a somewhat different composition and following, making its major appeal for support to the middle classes and nonunionized sections of the working class.

But it doesn't determine which interest controls, dominates, runs, and uses the Democratic Party. We say it is dominated, as the Republican Party is dominated, by a minority of its members—by a small group of monopoly capitalists who also control the economy, the government, the means of communication, and the educational system.

It doesn't matter what the Democratic platform says—the chief function of this party, as of the Republican Party, is to protect the interests of the monopoly capitalists at home and abroad. It doesn't matter what the candidates of this party *say* during election campaigns (they usually say what they think will win votes, not what they think)—what counts is what its officeholders *do* about the important issues of the day. Only a few examples are possible now:

The overwhelming majority of the people of this country, and of the members of both capitalist parties, want peace, the relaxation of international tensions, a ban on nuclear explosions, and so on. But what do they get? Wars, war crises, preparation for war, militarization, the draft, a permanent arms economy, and crushing taxes to maintain it; the continuation of the cold war and cold war propaganda. And the Democratic Party's chief complaint against the Republicans is that they don't appropriate and spend enough for these purposes! On this issue the Democratic Party surely serves the interests of the ruling class faithfully and consistently.

The Democrats differ from the Republicans occasionally on what to do about unemployment, because the Democrats usually have greater support among the unemployed and want to retain that support. But their differences are minor, sometimes insignificant. They agree on the basic things: that the present economic system must not be reorganized to abolish unemployment; that when workers are laid off through no fault of their own, *they* should suffer cuts in their living standards, rather than the employers; that jobless compensation should not be paid for the duration of unemployment; that the workweek should not be shortened. These are things the capitalist class thinks too.

The Jim Crow system in the U.S. is the scandal of the world. Nevertheless, the American ruling class shows no intention of abolishing it within the lifetime of anyone now living. In the South the Democratic Party is a one-party dictatorship dedicated to maintaining white supremacy. In Congress, it provides the bulk of the votes against meaningful civil rights legislation. Northern Democrats have to make some gestures to keep the Negro vote, but their liberalism is rarely more than skin-deep on this question. If you elect liberals like [Senators Philip] Hart and [Patrick] McNamara, who swear undying devotion to the civil rights cause, the first thing they do when they get to Washington is vote to elect the southern Democratic enemies of the Negro people to the key congressional posts, which are used to block civil rights and all other progressive legislation. Liberals like Governor Williams will make impassioned speeches about injustice to Negroes in the South, but no one has ever heard him utter a single word about the most Jim Crow city in the North—right on his own doorstep—Dearborn, whose mayor boasts that no Negro can live there. So it would be putting it mildly to say that the Democratic Party's policy on civil rights is in accord with that of the ruling class, which always benefits from hatred and discord among the workers.

My final example is civil liberties. We are still suffering from the effects of the witch-hunt launched to silence all opposition to the cold war. The record shows that the Democratic Party served the capitalist class just as zealously in this witch-hunt as the Republicans. The Democrats passed and enforced the Smith Act to gag political dissent. Democratic presidents transformed the FBI into a political police force. The Democrats started the misnamed government "loyalty" program. A Democratic president initiated the "subversive" blacklist. Democrats spearheaded the passage of the Internal Security Act of 1950. Liberal Democrats took the lead in passing the Humphrey-Butler "Communist Control" Act of 1954. We tend to think of this as the era of McCarthyism, but the Democrats, liberal as well as conservative, were in there doing their fair share of gnawing away at the Bill of Rights. And not only in Washington, but in Lansing too. The Trucks Law of 1952 was the worst and most repressive law ever passed in Michigan. All the Democrats in the legislature voted for it. Williams, begged by the civil libertarians to veto this bill that would turn Michigan into a police state, said he could see no reason not to sign it, and sign it he did. For the next four years he ignored all appeals that he call for its repeal. It would still be on the books if it had been left up to him rather than the U.S. Supreme Court, which finally struck it down.

Having given an analysis of the Democratic Party, for better or worse, I want to indicate now why it is wrong from just about every conceivable angle for progressives to work in it. I'll take up the labor movement first, the radical groups second.

Unions are created in the first place because there is a fundamental clash of interests between workers and capitalists. A necessary condition for the effective functioning of unions is that they be independent of the capitalists; as we all know, a company union, an organization dominated by the employers, does not and cannot defend the workers' interests. I believe it can be stated as a law: the more independent a union is of capitalists, of individual capitalists and of the capitalist class as a whole, the better able it is to defend the workers' interests. Or if you don't care for the word *law*, let me put it this way: Independence of the labor movement is a first principle, recognized and expounded by the best union leaders, like Debs and Haywood.

This has always been true, but it is especially true today, when the monopoly stage of capitalism expands the role of the state and gives all struggles, including labor struggles, an openly political character. What labor in our country needs above everything else is a party of its own, which can fight for the needs and aspirations of the workers on the political field as unions can on the economic field. (The present steel negotiations show how inseparable these two fields are becoming.)

But instead of having a party of its own, the labor movement is dependent, in the political sphere, on a party controlled by the capitalists and promoting the interests of the capitalists. It is a tail to the Democratic kite, as one union leader put it. This must be designated as a violation of the principle of independence on the basis of which the union movement was created. It is not only wrong in principle, however. It is also harmful in practice, and the cause of most of the ills besetting the labor movement today.

It was reported not long ago that the unions spent more money on the last congressional election than the Democratic campaign committees did. What have they gotten in return? UAW Secretary-Treasurer Emil Mazey said about a month ago: "We won an election last November but until now we have not received a single thing from this victory." This is true after *every* election.

The present Congress, controlled by the Democrats the unions helped to elect, has refused to end the filibuster. It has refused to extend jobless compensation for a year. It is on the verge of passing the Kennedy-Ervin bill to further restrict the independence of the unions by subjecting them to government control, a bill which becomes worse and worse every time Congress takes it up. And at the recent conference on unemployment in Washington, all the AFL-CIO could get from the leaders of the Democratic Party was a promise to study the question.

No wonder Jack Crellin of the *Detroit Times* commented after the jobless conference that the AFL-CIO seems to be getting a "mighty poor return on its investment." And, he added ironically, "At least Jimmy Hoffa gets six per cent on his."

Hoffa is not our idea of a model labor leader, any more than Reuther is. But sometimes they tell the truth too. I think Hoffa did that in a recent interview with the *Detroit Free Press*. Asked to comment on the alliance between the UAW and the Michigan Democratic Party, he said: "The UAW has less power that way. If I got you, I don't have to worry about you. The Democrats control the UAW in Michigan. Reuther has got himself into a trap and doesn't know how to get out." Reuther knows how to get out all right, but except for that, I think Hoffa's statement comes close to the truth, which I would put this way: Thanks to this alliance, the Democrats have much more influence in the labor movement than the labor movement has in the Democratic Party.

The Democrats can take the unions for granted, because they feel they have them in their pocket; because the unions, having sworn not to create their own party, have nowhere else to go. Who can deny this? Dixiecrats get more concessions from the Democrats than the union leaders do because they threaten to bolt and form their own party. The union leaders not only have become dependent on the Democratic Party, they have become its captives. And this is one of the reasons why the Democratic Party has been moving steadily to the right year after year. So labor's support of the Democrats is wrong in all respects—from the standpoint of principle, from the pragmatic standpoint of results.

What the labor movement and its allies need is to make a clean break with both capitalist parties and form an independent labor party dedicated to winning control of the government and putting into effect a program that will meet the needs of the majority of the people.

For radicals and socialists, the situation is even more clear-cut. Our goal—the creation of a new society through working-class political action—requires that we help the labor movement to break away from capitalist parties and capitalist politics; and that we expand the influence and organization of radical and revolutionary groups and parties fit to provide leadership to the workers in a fight for a better society.

Neither of these objectives can be served by working in the Democratic Party. Again, it is wrong in principle and wrong in every other way that can be measured. The highways are littered with the political corpses of radicals and socialists who entered the Democratic Party with the idea of making it radical, and who ended up by becoming mere liberals or even conservatives themselves.

The main function of the radical movement today is educational and propagandistic, pending the time—not as distant as some radicals think—when it once again can lead the people in great actions and struggles. To educate means first of all to say what is, to tell the people the truth. What good is a radical, what right has he to any hearing, if he doesn't meet this minimum condition?

But you can't be in the Democratic Party and tell the truth to the people. The first thing demanded of you in the Democratic Party is that you support its candidates, that is, help spread the propaganda that the election of Democrats is in the interests of the people. If you do this, you have to lie, you have to cover up the fact that the Democratic Party stands for the cold war, more armaments, little or no help to the unemployed, racial oppression, restrictions on the Bill of Rights, retention of the Taft-Hartley Act, maintenance of the status quo generally.

In short, the condition for working in the Democratic Party is that you must abdicate the primary function of the radical. If everyone did it, it would mean the death of all organized radical opposition to capitalism.

The final test of a policy is in its results. The policy we are debating tonight is not a new one, and it has been tested for a long time. The labor movement has been working in and supporting the Democratic Party for the last twenty-five years: Isn't it true, Brother Haessler, that the Democratic Party today stands to the right of where it stood twenty-five years ago, and not to the left? The main sections of the radical movement have been supporting the Democratic Party, directly or indirectly, with only a few lapses, for over twenty years: Can you claim, Brother Haessler, that radical influence in the Democratic Party is greater than it was twenty years ago? Can you claim that radical influence in the country is generally greater today than it was in the days when the radical parties considered it their duty to oppose the Democratic Party at the polls?

Supporting the Democratic Party is at best an exercise in futility for radicals, and one of the causes contributing to their decline. At worst, it is a betrayal of anticapitalist principles that are at the heart of radicalism, and without which it must decay and die.

It is also a repudiation of the whole past of American radicalism. If it's right to support the Democrats today, if it's wrong to oppose them at the polls and to work in every other way to expose their reactionary character, then everything the old socialist movement did in its best days was also wrong and should be renounced rather than pointed to as an inspiration for the future. If it's right to support the Democrats today, then Debs was wrong in helping to organize the Socialist Party in running those magnificent election campaigns, in teaching that it is unprincipled for socialists to support capitalist candidates; then Debs was just a hopeless sectarian, whose example has little to offer us today. (Which, incidentally, is what William Z. Foster and the Communist Party now are saying.)

Speaking of Debs reminds me of the question that people sometimes ask: What happened to the old idealism of the socialist movement, the self-sacrificing spirit of solidarity and militancy that the American radical movement used to know? What happened to it was that the leaders of the movement, lacking or losing confidence in the capacity of the workers to change society and govern themselves, began to find all kinds of pretexts and rationalizations for deserting the policies of class struggle and embracing the policies of class collaboration. One of the manifestations of this change was the change from the old principle that it's the duty of socialists to oppose capitalist party candidates, to run independent candidates and use election campaigns to expose the nature of capitalism and present the truth about socialism—a change from this tradition to arguments that independent campaigns achieve nothing, that you must not let yourself get "isolated," that you must adjust yourself to the politics of the labor bureaucrats rather than fight them.

You can't create idealism, you can't maintain militancy and devotion to the great goals of the socialist future through such maneuvers. Take the workers into the Democratic swamp of opportunism, horse trades, and dirty machine politics, where any piece of filthy work is justified if it helps win the next election, and you can't expect anything but that it will sap the workers' militancy, devotion to principle, and class-consciousness—if they remain there and don't drop out of politics altogether demoralized.

The future lies with the youth—the young people just beginning to recover from a decade of cold war conformism. They've heard enough lies to last them for a lifetime. What they need is the truth, simple and direct. Only if they get it will they respond with those reserves of militancy and bravery that are especially characteristic of the young, that seem to be the prerequisite of every genuine revolution, and that can revitalize American radicalism as an effective fighting force. You'll get nowhere feeding the youth white lies or half-truths about the Democratic Party. You'll be shirking your duty to them and to the future if you tell them to go work in the Democratic Party.

Therefore, the policy dictated to progressives is to oppose the Democratic Party, not to work in it or get others to support it. Those of us who are workers should strive in our unions to bring about a break with capitalist politics, and the formation of an independent labor party. Those of us who are radicals and socialists should do everything we can to fight the two-party system, utilize election campaigns to spread socialist ideas and influence, and run socialist slates for office, if possible along the general lines of the Independent-Socialist ticket in New York in 1958.

That ticket, bringing together independent radicals, former Progressive Party members, and Socialist Workers Party members in a united socialist campaign against both capitalist parties, was an encouraging progressive alternative to the compromising, demoralizing, self-defeating policy of working in the Democratic Party. The Socialist Workers Party advocated similar united left-wing tickets here in Michigan in the 1957 and 1958 election campaigns. The other radical groups in the state rejected its proposals in those years. We hope they will respond differently to proposals for a united ticket of radicals, socialists, and progressives in the 1960 campaign, nationally and locally. If they don't we promise we will still try to act as socialists should, by placing a socialist ticket on the ballot in Michigan and running a campaign that will help promote independent working class political action by openly telling the truth about capitalism and socialism.

REBUTTALS

HAESSLER: Let me say first that many of the things that Brother Breitman said about the Democratic Party as a whole are true enough. And I had no thought of denying that when I presented the case. What I was arguing was effective political action as against propaganda action, and I notice that one of the most significant things that Brother Breitman said was that for some time to come radical third party action would have to be of a propagandistic nature.

The Democratic Party is regarded by my opponent as one of the few things in the world that doesn't change. Everything else is changing, even the Republican Party; some of the Republicans are liberal, vote in the senate on the liberal side. But the Democratic Party does not change. It's a stinking mess of corruption and reaction. Just summarizing in three words what we've heard for the last thirty minutes. Now that is obviously an exaggeration. It's permissible in partisan debate, and I won't try to knock it down. I notice that nothing was said by Brother Breitman with regard to my opening point. Which was the capture of the Michigan Supreme Court by the labor-backed and labor-financed Democratic Party.

Certainly Governor Williams signed the Trucks Act. The Republican state supreme court upheld the Trucks Act, and then it went to the U.S. Supreme Court; and the U.S. Supreme Court knocked it out. Did one person go to jail in the meantime under the Trucks Act? Was one person fined in the meantime? Very effective debating, Brother Breitman, but let's have all the facts. And so we can take up other things that were mentioned.

Certainly in the U.S. government President Truman started the loyalty program for government employees. But why did he do it? I don't know if he should have done it even in view of all the facts, but the reason he did it was that McCarthy and his gang, both Democrat and Republican, in the Senate, were starting a witch-hunt, and Truman, mistakenly or not, thought that this loyalty program was one way to stop it. It wasn't that Truman's heart was in the red-baiting campaign, but you know McCarthy's heart was there, and Truman, as well as those who advised him, thought that this was one way to put a brake on the witch-hunt movement. Of course, people suffered; they would have suffered even more if this hadn't been put up. But it was not, as Brother Breitman says, one of the worst smells of the Democratic Party in Washington. It was an attempt to keep a bad thing in check.

So I think we would proceed more fruitfully in this matter if we came down to cases in our own state, where things are getting along pretty well. Of course you say that the Democrats rule labor in this state. Nobody thinks so except the speaker and a few of those who agreed with him beforehand. The whole complaint in this state, in the press, in private party councils of the Republicans and of the old-line Democrats themselves, is not that the Democrats have captured the UAW and its sister unions, but the other way around. Who is the national committeeman from Michigan? Is he a labor man, or a prolabor man, or is he an old-line Democrat? Who got the biggest vote of all the candidates in the spring election for public office? Was it an old-line Democrat or was it Brother Woodcock, vice-president and crown prince of the UAW, a man who used to be on the National Executive Committee of the Socialist Party? Those are the kind of Democrats that own the party in this state.

And my program to you is that there are other states emerging into a similar situation, where organized labor is strong enough, where it has the money to put up, which talks in political campaigns, as our splinter parties know only too well (they could talk a lot louder if they had a lot more money). Those are the things that are promising and those are the things that the youth of our country, if they are interested organizationally, politically, and not just as a pure sect of propagandists, if they're interested in getting things done politically, helping to guide their course, that's the kind of direction that the youth interested in political action should take.

Now I've heard, and I used to spout it myself, and I believed it for many, many years, that what Brother Breitman has proposed tonight is the true course. I no longer think so. We have to recognize conditions in this country, that it's the two-party system, very hard to overthrow, that you start working politically effectively by getting into that party, and you realize that the national party doesn't mean anything except once in four years. It's a coalition of state machines, and when you begin to get your hand in the state machine, you're getting to be one of the little levers, and then you and your friends reach out and get hold of bigger levers, and finally you control the whole thing. You get into that Democratic car, and when the time comes, you grab the wheel and then you run it. You run it the way you and your other labor members want it run, and then the Michigan car, the New Jersey car, and the Minnesota car, and the California car, and the Pennsylvania car, and the West Virginia car and all the others, then you get together, you'll have a national fleet of cars. Not run by old-line Democrats.

In fact, enlightened northern Democrats have begun to realize that the party doesn't need the Dixiecrats in order to win nationally. They're telling them to go to hell. And the Dixiecrats aren't doing it. You watch 1960, the Dixiecrats know they can no longer run the Democratic Party but they know that by the seniority system, which Brother Breitman thinks is so terrible, the Dixiecrats can still hang on to certain committee chairmanships. They now have both the Speaker of the House and the majority leader of the Senate. But what did those two men do just a few months ago? They formally severed their connection with the Dixiecrat caucus, the southern group, and affiliated with the western caucus. Both Speaker [Sam] Rayburn and Senate majority leader [Lyndon B.] Johnson. Now Brother Breitman may think they did this with the fell intent of running the western states. My opinion is that they climbed on a bandwagon. And in time, Rayburn, who is way up in his seventies, will retire on a fat pension, or he'll die. Other southerners will die, too, some will get defeated by younger men, the chairmanships will go around, and you take a freshman senator like Hart, coming up to Washington and asking for his committee appointments, and he's apt to be in the Senate for a long time. I know he married a millionairess—the daughter of a sweatshop manufacturer of the worst odor in Detroit, the late Mr. Briggs, who used to pay his women ten cents an hour and cheat them on overtime. Well, Briggs isn't in control, and I doubt whether Miss Briggs, now Mrs. Hart, controls Hart himself. I know that Hart has wrong things about him, I know that in the last campaign he bragged he was one of those who red-baited against the Communist Party. Of course, all sorts of people have red-baited against the Communist Party; Norman Thomas has done it as effectively as Walter Reuther has done it. But that's political opportunism and not conviction. Because one of the grievances that the Socialist Party in my opinion has against the reds, against the Communists, is that the Communists have made a going concern of a number of countries and the Socialists never have. But that's just family bickering, apart from the main course tonight. What should a progressive who is interested in organized political action do? Should he work in the Democratic Party? Yes, that's what I repeat for George's rebuttal.

BREITMAN: When Brother Haessler says that the Democratic Party can become a labor-dominated party, he puts me in the position of trying to prove a negative, which is a difficult thing to do. On the bus the other day I overheard two teenagers: One asked if the other believed in ghosts. The second said, "No, there are no such things." The first said, "How can you say that when you can't prove it? Go ahead, prove that there are no ghosts." All the second could do was mutter that you can't prove the moon isn't made of green cheese either.

It's hard to prove a negative to the satisfaction of all. I've tried to show how the unions and many radicals have been working for a long time to move the Democratic Party to the left, and all that's happened is that it's moved to the right. I say it's your job to disprove that. Or to show why efforts to reform the Democratic Party will have any different results now than they had in the past. It's not enough to merely assert that the Democratic Party can be changed from an instrument of the capitalist class into an instrument of the working class—you have to demonstrate this possibility by current developments and trends, by logic, by the lessons of experience, which I've tried to use.

But Brother Haessler makes my job easier when he claims that the Democratic Party already has changed, and already has "for all practical purposes" been captured by labor in Michigan, among other states. This is a question of fact which all of you can test for yourselves. Let me cite a few of the many examples you will find showing that the labor movement, far from controlling the Democratic Party in this or any other state, is a captive of the Democratic Party; is a prisoner of the Williamses and the Staeblers; is the tail, not the dog.

Just four months ago the Michigan AFL-CIO decided to conduct a fight for a state law to pay unemployment compensation for the duration of unemployment. This was a big step forward for the labor movement. They showed they were serious when they got the Democratic minority leader in Lansing and other Democrats in the House to agree to sponsor and introduce the bill. Then Williams stepped in. He didn't attack the bill directly, just said that it was different from what he favored, and he would have to study it. But that did it. The Democrats in Lansing backed away on the double. Not one of them would introduce the bill after that. The AFL-CIO helped to elect sixty-seven Democrats now in Lansing, but not one of them will even introduce this bill. However, that's not the worst part; the most miserable thing of all is that the AFL-CIO then dropped the proposal too—its own proposal. They don't advocate in May what they said was necessary in January. Three days ago the AFL-CIO held a conference in Lansing on unemployment, and failed to even mention this bill that they said was necessary in January—even mention it as one of their long-range objectives. Labor supplies the money and the votes to elect the Democrats, but the Democrats have a greater voice in determining labor's program than labor has in determining the Democrats'.

Another example of who's captured whom: We in Michigan pay among the highest consumer taxes in the country. The Democratic platforms of 1948, 1950, 1952, 1954, pledged opposition to additional consumer taxes. In January 1955, the Republicans introduced a road construction program involving an increase of 2¢ a gallon in the consumer tax paid on gasoline. The CIO denounced this plan. So did Williams. He called it a "political plunderbund," and said, "It almost made me gag." Almost—but not quite. Because less than a month later, he accepted a so-called compromise in which the added consumer tax was set at 1½¢ rather than 2¢. The CIO then dropped its opposition to added consumer taxes. And its members in the legislature voted for the increase. Of course if a Republican governor had violated his platform in such a fashion, the CIO would have denounced him from hell to breakfast as a man whose promises were worthless, whose platform wasn't worth the paper it was printed on.

But that's not the point I'm trying to make now. The point is, this is another example of how the labor movement's own program becomes conservatized as a result of its alliance with the Democrats, another example showing who is the master in this alliance. You are urged to be practical, but I really can't think of anything more utopian than the idea of trying to capture the Democratic Party away from its bosses. It's not a democratic organization controlled by its members. It is a highly bureaucratic structure dominated from the top. You can't take it away from its bosses. If you did in this or that isolated case, you'd either be expelled or the antilabor elements would walk out and get the recognition of the national party. And you would end up having "captured" only yourselves.

The second thing to understand about this is that the union leaders don't want to capture the Democratic Party. They're as much against capturing the Democratic Party as they are against forming a labor party, because they don't want labor to have its own party, no matter how it originates. Until 1952, the CIO delegates at the Michigan State Democratic Convention used to meet in a caucus to discuss what they, the CIO delegates, were going to do. But at the spring convention in 1952, some of them talked incautiously about "taking over." Well, they were quickly squelched by Gus Scholle, who told them, "You won't capture anyone but yourselves." Since 1952, the labor delegates at the Democratic convention no longer even meet as a caucus, as a separate group. They have less intention of "taking over" than ever before. My point here is, you'll have just as big a fight on your hands trying to get the unions to capture the Democratic Party as you will in trying to get them to decide to form a labor party. The difference is, when you win the labor movement to a labor party, you'll have something, while if you finally succeed in getting the unions to try to take over the Democratic Party, you'll have accomplished little, because the Democratic Party won't let itself be captured. From a purely practical standpoint, which has been invoked here, it is far more realistic to keep fighting inside the unions for a labor party than to try to make the unions try to capture the Democratic Party.

Brother Haessler speaks about great accomplishments from labor infiltration of the Democratic Party in Michigan. He spoke on it at some length, but in the end he had only one concrete example of an accomplishment, and that was the decision of the Michigan Supreme Court on unemployment compensation. But this decision is not really as remarkable as he says. All it provides is that under certain conditions, workers laid off as a result of a strike in other states shall be eligible for unemployment compensation. But, according to Williams and the UAW, around thirty-five other states in the country already have provisions similar to that. And nobody would seriously claim that their having such provisions is the result of the Democratic Party or courts being controlled by the labor movement in those states.

Brother Haessler asks if this could have been done through any other force than the Democratic Party; if it could be done by the Socialist Workers Party or any of the other small radical groups at the present time. Obviously the answer is no. They are not in a position now to get a majority of the state supreme court. But it doesn't follow that labor therefore is forced to rely on the Democratic Party. It can get concessions of this modest caliber by exerting mass pressure on both capitalist parties, without supporting either. And it can get much bigger concessions by forming its own party to fight both old parties. The alternative should not be restricted to the small radical parties of today or the Democratic Party of today; the choice for progressives is also between the Democratic Party of today and the labor party that the union movement is now capable of building.

Brother Haessler points to the difficulties of building a

labor party. I think he overstates them. The labor movement in the United States is big enough to build its own party; it is bigger than the labor movement in other countries that have labor parties. It can do it if it wants to. In its very first election, a labor party would sweep the big cities in the United States. Here in Detroit it could elect five or six labor congressmen to replace the Democrats. It could do this in all the other big cities too. From the very beginning it could have in Congress a large bloc of congressmen who would fight for the things labor wants, and which it doesn't have there now. From the start it would emerge as the second party, rather than a third party, because the Democratic Party minus the labor movement will amount to very little. What's lacking for this is not personnel, what's lacking is not the people with the experience to run such a party, or to be its candidates, or to get it on the ballot, or to do its precinct work. What's lacking is the will, which is paralyzed by the opposition of the top union leaders. The job of progressives in the labor movement is to fight to crystallize that will by opposing the political policies of the leadership, not to support and aid them.

    I might say, if we're going to mention "all the facts," that Justice George Edwards, who is presented here as something of a hero because he spent thirty days in jail as a union organizer in 1937, also has another achievement in his record—namely that in 1949, as president of the Detroit City Council, he was the one who introduced and pushed for the passage of the reactionary City Loyalty Investigating Committee. And it is Edwards, among others, who is pointed to as one of the bulwarks of liberalism on the supreme court. It is like the attempt here to defend the Democrats pushing through witch-hunt measures on the ground that they were trying to prevent the Republicans from pushing through worse witch-hunt measures, which seems to me to be carrying the argument of the "lesser evil" to the point of absurdity.

I was interested by Brother Haessler's advice to Reuther to abandon the Socialist Party, and avoid those "entangling little alliances." Reuther was to some extent perhaps persuaded by him; at any rate we know he left the Socialist Party for substantially such reasons. The trouble is that he got engaged instead in one big alliance, with the Democratic Party, and it's that in which the labor movement is badly entangled and hamstrung.

For progressives to spend their time and effort working in the Democratic Party is neither progressive nor practical. This policy does not result in teaching workers that they cannot trust capitalist politicians and parties. Instead, it results in strengthening illusions that the Democratic Party is a lesser evil, and that they can solve their problems through that party rather than needing a new party. It does not educate the workers to act along the lines of class struggle in politics. On the contrary, it encourages and justifies the continuation of class collaboration in politics. You cannot serve the cause of socialism and progress by telling the workers that the Democrats are worthy of support despite their procapitalist, prowar, pro–witch-hunt, pro–Jim Crow program. Therefore, we appeal to Carl Haessler and all other progressives who favor spending their considerable talents in the Democratic Party to reconsider.

The world tide is now against capitalism. Workers have ended it in many parts of the world. In the United States too, incurable sicknesses are coming to the fore—growing discontent with foreign policy, a new permanent army of unemployed, a deepening demand for integration, an intense restlessness and instability. New opportunities are about to open up for radicals. Let us try to work together to meet them. We still have differences among ourselves. Without denying them or forgetting them, let us work together in those areas where we see eye to eye—in our political opposition to war, depression, racial oppression, infringements of civil liberties. Let us get together on these issues, and do in 1960 what the progressives and socialists did in New York last year: Let us put in the field a united Independent-Socialist ticket that will challenge both capitalist parties and educate all the people that it can reach to understand the necessity for a new party and a new society.

HAESSLER: I have a few minutes in what you might call re-rebuttal. I haven't anything to say against Brother Breitman's peroration. I think the ideals expressed are noble; are ideals that I agree with. I further have nothing to say against his appeals for certain people to devote themselves to the organizing of an independent labor party. If they wish to, let them do it. And let me say further that I myself am not enough interested in political organization work to work in the Democratic Party. What I've been presenting is a practical program for those who are politically, organizationally interested. If you want to work and achieve practical political results in this state and a number of other states, do it through the Democratic Party. Don't waste your time trying to achieve practical results in these nonexistent or barely existent third parties of all sorts. That's all I was proposing.

To come down to a few trivial points, I didn't parade George Edwards as a hero; he's not one of my heroes. I was simply showing the course of evolution by labor control of the Democratic Party in this state. Here was a jailbird, in jail for the contempt of the courts in our state. He is now sitting on the topmost court in the state, and bawling out lower judges for not acting in a progressive manner. It was just an incident in political evolution, and not a parade of my heroes. In fact, I haven't mentioned any of my heroes tonight. Brother Breitman has—Eugene Debs was one of my long-time heroes, and the first picture ever taken of my first baby was when Debs held him in his arms. I sent that off to the relatives at Christmas time, and one of them replied,

"We're so glad to see a picture of your baby, but please send us next time a picture that we can love."

Well, as for the future, I want to see a land of plenty, a land of peace, a land of happiness. I want to see the dreams come true of the couples with two incomes in the family, the wife working too, and she saying, "When we get rich, I want to have a vacuum cleaner upstairs as well as downstairs," and the man says, "Yes, Sally, when we get rich, I want to use a blue blade, both edges on one shave." And the time will come when those dreams will be realized, and many bigger dreams than those. I'm for a practical third party. I don't want you to waste your time on any if it's not going to be practical. If you want to be practical in an organizationally political way in this state, and in a number of other states, the practical and effective way is, as I've said, through the transforming of the Democratic Party.

Index

Abolitionists, 24–25
Abortion, 22, 43–44, 45
Abrams, Henry, 97
Adams, Clark, 123
AFL-CIO (American Federation of Labor-Congress of Industrial Organizations), 30, 135
AFL-CIO (Michigan), 120, 144–45
AFSCME (American Federation of State, County and Municipal Employees), 12
Altgeld, John Peter, 77
American Car and Foundry, 129
American Federation of Labor, 81
American Labor Party, 73, 74, 86, 98, 127
Amnesty, 22
Anti-Semitism, 49–50
Antiwar demonstrations (1965): April 17, 58, 60, 81, 85; October 15–16, 58, 79, 85; November 27, 58, 83
Antiwar movement, 21, 26, 45, 47, 58, 97, 115; and coalitionism, 61–62, 66, 70; strategy for, 109–12
Aronowitz, Stanley, 9, 57, 76, 90, 97; on antiwar movement, 79, 82–83, 84–85, 109–10; on Committee for Independent Political Action, 101–4; on Democratic Party, 104–8; on early Socialist Party, 77–79, 90–92, 113–15

Barnes, Jack, 9, 57, 79, 84, 86, 105, 117; on antiwar movement, 110–12; on coalitionism, 59–63, 68, 70, 74; on Committee for Independent Political Action, 96–100; on Democratic Party, 63, 67–69; on early Socialist Party, 91–93; on independent political action, 72–73
Beame, Abraham, 12, 31–32, 33, 38, 39, 104
Berger, Victor, 77
Bill of Rights, 136–37
Bismarck, Otto von, 115
Bolsheviks, 48
Booth, Paul, 102, 117
Boston, 34
Brecht, Bertolt, 16
Breitman, George, 9, 119; on Democratic Party, 129–39; on labor movement, 134–36, 144–47; on labor party, 134, 146–48
Bridges, Harry, 126–27
Buckley, William, 65, 98, 101
Burton, Phil, 105

Calley, William, 22
Camejo, Peter, 10, 11, 12, 14, 20, 21, 53–55, 69; on antiwar movement, 22, 26, 45; on Black movement, 26–27, 33–34, 35–36; on Democratic Party, 25–26, 27–28, 40–41, 42, 48–49; on Middle East, 49–50; on New York City budget crisis, 23–24, 32–33, 36–37; on women's movement, 45
Cannon, James P., 78
Carey, Hugh, 12, 31–32, 38
Carter, Jimmy, 12, 19–20, 21, 24, 25–27, 45, 46, 54, 55; and big business, 15, 38–39; and Blacks, 33, 34; compared to Ford, 14, 17, 30, 43, 44; and "ethnic purity,"

153

26–27; and Hawkins-Humphrey bill, 27–28, 40; and New York City budget crisis, 32, 38; program of, 16–20, 22–23; and unemployment, 27–28, 40, 44–45; and Vietnam War, 22; and women, 43–44; and working class, 16, 23, 28–29, 48
CIO (Congress of Industrial Organizations), 66–67, 68, 86, 118
CIO (Michigan), 144–46
City University of New York, 12, 20, 36–37, 38, 54
Civil liberties, 132–33
Civil rights, 132
Civil rights movement, 21, 62, 66, 97
Coalitionism, 59–60, 61–63, 68–70, 74
Coalition of Labor Union Women (CLUW), 44
Cohelan, Jeffrey, 105
Committee for Independent Political Action (CIPA), 9, 58, 93–94, 95–100; program of, 101, 117–18
Communist Party (Indonesia), 75
Communist Party (Italy), 93
Communist Party (U.S.), 46, 47, 58, 78, 80, 93, 104, 117, 138; support to Democrats, 59, 65–66, 67, 68, 74
Community Party, 74
Congressional Black Caucus, 44
Crellin, Jack, 135
Crystal City (Texas), 29

Death penalty, 22–23
DeBerry, Clifton, 58, 69
Debs, Eugene V., 47, 77, 79, 92, 98, 112, 134, 137–38, 150
Democratic Party, 7, 20, 21–22, 25–26, 28–29, 30, 31, 33, 58, 71, 80, 94–95, 118, 122–23, 143–44, 149, 150, 151; and Blacks, 34, 61–63, 64–65, 66, 130, 132; character of,

68, 72, 130–31; and civil liberties, 132–33, 140–41, 148–49; and civil rights, 132; coalition in, 58, 59–60, 66, 67–74, 95, 117, 130–31; compared to Republicans, 131–32, 140–41; composition of, 13, 39, 40–41, 130; and early Socialist Party, 73, 74, 112–13; and labor, 52, 53, 65–66, 133–36, 143–48; in Michigan, 123–25; and New York City budget crisis, 23–24, 38; 1976 convention, 44; primary of, 93–96, 98–99, 102–4, 106–8; program of, 27–28; and radicals, 136–39; reform wing of, 95–96, 99, 100, 101–2; and unemployment, 17; and Vietnam War, 41, 43, 51–52, 60–61, 63–64; and war, 46, 48, 131
Democratic Socialist Organizing Committee (DSOC), 9–10, 14, 26, 31, 32, 50; and Democratic Party, 20, 21
DeSapio, Carmine, 94–95
Detroit City Council, 148
Detroit Free Press, 135
Detroit Times, 135
Dixiecrats, 71, 135, 142–43
Dole, Robert, 17–18

Eastern Europe, 113–14
Edwards, George, 124, 148, 150
Eisenhower, Dwight, 64, 120, 127
Election laws, 42–43
Equal Rights Amendment, 44, 46
"Ethnic purity," 26–27

Farmer-Labor Democratic Party (Minnesota), 126
FBI, 41
Ferry, W.H., 61
First International, 15
Ford, Gerald, 20, 22, 25, 27, 32, 54, 55; and big business, 15, 16; compared

to Carter, 14, 17, 20–21, 24, 30, 34, 41, 43–44, 45; and New York City budget crisis, 32, 38
Ford Motor Company, 123
Fortune, 15
Foster, William Z., 138
Freedom Democratic Party (Mississippi) (MFDP), 58, 85, 88, 94, 100
Free tuition, 38
Friday Night Socialist Forum (Detroit), 120
Full Employment Act (1948), 27–28
Fund for the Republic, 61

Gilligan, John, 55
Gitlin, Todd, 102
Goldwater, Barry, 28, 58, 65, 66, 71; on Vietnam War, 59, 60–61, 64
Gompers, Samuel, 81
Gotbaum, Victor, 12, 31–33
Gulf of Tonkin resolution, 51

Haessler, Carl, 9, 119; on Democratic Party, 121–29, 137, 140–44, 147, 149, 150–51
Harding, Warren, 77
Harrington, Michael, 9–10, 11, 14, 21, 29, 30, 31, 32, 33, 34, 35, 40, 45–46, 52–53, 116; and antiwar movement, 26, 43; on Carter, 38; on Democratic Party, 23, 28, 33, 39–40; on Middle East, 50
Hart, Philip, 132
Hawkins-Humphrey bill, 18, 27, 39, 40–41, 46
Hayden, Tom, 102
Haywood, Bill, 91, 134
Hillquit, Morris, 76–77, 78
Hiroshima, 48
Hitler, Adolf, 25, 26
Hoffa, Jimmy, 120, 125, 135
Housing discrimination, 27
Humphrey, Hubert, 85
Humphrey-Butler "Communist Control" Act (1954), 133
Hungarian revolution, 115

Independent political action, 72–73
Independent-Socialist ticket, 120, 139, 150
Industrial unionism, 66–67
Industrial Workers of the World (IWW), 77–78
Internal Security Act (1950), 133
International Brotherhood of Teamsters, 120
International Workingmen's Association, 15
Ireland, Douglas, 70
Israel, 49–50

Japanese-Americans, 48
Jim Crow, 132
Johnson, Andrew, 38
Johnson, Lyndon B., 18, 28, 64, 65, 66, 71, 143; and Vietnam War, 36, 37, 41, 43, 58, 59–61, 64, 82

Kefauver, Estes, 65
Kennedy, Edward, 51
Kennedy, John F., 18, 66
Kennedy, Robert, 43, 51
Kennedy-Corman bill, 19
Kennedy-Ervin bill, 134–35
Kent State (May 1970), 55
Kissinger, Clark, 117
Korean War, 47, 120
Kosygin, Alexei, 96

Labor movement (U.S.), 15–16, 21, 23
Labor party, 30, 134, 147–48
Labor's Giant Step (Preis), 80
La Follette, Robert M., Sr., 122
Lenin, Vladimir Ilyich, 34, 35, 98
Lewis, Denny, 125
Lewis, John L., 80, 118, 125
Liberal Party (New York), 106, 127

Liberation, 61
Lincoln, Abraham, 37–38
Lipset, Seymour Martin, 81
London, Meyer, 77
Lynd, Staughton, 61–62, 66, 70, 72

McCarthy, Eugene, 30–31, 42, 43, 51, 126
McCarthy, Joseph, 120, 140–41
McNamara, Patrick, 132
McReynolds, David, 58, 64–65, 69
Malcolm X, 65
Mao Tse-tung, 93
March on Washington (April 17, 1965), 60, 81, 85
Marx, Karl, 15, 34–35, 39
Max, Steve, 70
Mazey, Emil, 134
Meany, George, 19
Medicare, 43
Mensheviks, 46–47
Middle East, 49–50
Militant, The, 9, 12, 28, 128
Militant Labor Forum (New York City), 64
Murphy, Frank, 47
Murray, Philip, 80
Mussolini, Benito, 25

Nagasaki, 48
National Civic Federation, 115
National Coordinating Committee to End the War in Vietnam, 79
National Guard, 22
National Guardian, 58, 59
National Liberation Front (Vietnam), 115–16
National Student Association, 102
Nazi movement, 26, 47
New Deal, 17–18, 100
New Left, 74, 80
New York City budget crisis, 12, 23–24, 31–32, 36, 38
Nixon, Richard, 18, 49, 65

Old Left, 74, 80
Open admissions, 38

Palestine Liberation Organization (PLO), 50
Palestinians, 49–50
Peace Party, 74
Potter, Paul, 81, 102, 117–18
Preis, Art, 80, 113
Progressive Party (1912), 77
Progressive Party (1924), 122
Progressive Party (1948), 73, 74, 122, 139

Radical movement, 81–84
Rayburn, Sam, 143
Raza Unida Party, 29
Reed, John, 78
Reid, Willie Mae, 12
Republican Party, 25, 27, 28, 29, 31, 32, 46, 52, 94, 106, 118, 122, 140, 141; compared to Democrats, 63–64, 68–69, 131–32
Reuther, Walter, 47, 120, 124–25, 143, 149
Revolutionary Student Brigade (RSB), 34
Rhodes, James, 55
Right-to-work laws, 23
Rockefeller, Nelson, 103
Roosevelt, Franklin D., 17–18, 46, 47, 48, 68, 73
Roosevelt, Theodore, 77
Russian revolution, 78, 92, 115
Rustin, Bayard, 58, 65, 70–71, 76, 81–82, 101, 116; on coalitionism, 60, 61–63, 66, 79–80, 104
Ruthenberg, Charles, 78
Ryan, William F., 104

Sadlowski, Ed, 30
SANE (Committee for a Sane Nuclear Policy), 58, 109
Scholle, August, 120, 146

SDS (Students for a Democratic Society), 9, 58, 87, 102
Senate (U.S.), 141, 142–43
Slavery, 24–25
SNCC (Student Nonviolent Coordinating Committee), 87, 110
Socialist Party (France), 93
Socialist Party (U.S.), 47, 67, 77–80, 86, 87, 117, 124–25, 141, 143, 149; before 1920, 90–92, 93, 112–13, 114, 115, 137–38; and Democratic Party, 74, 112–13
Socialist Workers Party (SWP), 7, 9, 10, 12, 34, 38, 58, 63, 104, 124, 128–29, 139; compared to Democrats, 39–40; on election tactics, 98–99, 120; on fascism, 48; on New York City budget crisis, 23–24; perspectives of, 117; program of, 14, 15, 16, 17–18, 21, 45, 46; on Vietnam War, 28
State capitalism, 113
Stevenson, Adlai, 65
Studies on the Left, 9, 100
Sukarno, 93
Supreme court (Michigan), 123–24, 140, 147, 148
Supreme Court (U.S.), 18, 44, 45, 46, 133, 140
Swope, Gerard, 115

Taft-Hartley Act (1947), 137
Thomas, Norman, 58, 60, 124, 143

Trucks Law (Michigan, 1952), 133, 140
Truman, Harry S., 80, 120, 140–41
Two-party system, 7, 142

Unemployment, 27–28, 29
United Auto Workers (UAW), 19, 120, 124, 134, 135, 141
United Mine Workers, 125–26

Vietnam (North), 59
Vietnam Day Committee (VDC), 102
Vietnam War, 18, 22, 24, 28, 29, 45, 47, 58, 62; and Democratic Party, 51–52; and Lyndon Johnson, 36, 37, 41, 43, 59–61; movement against, 21, 26, 45, 47, 58, 97, 115–16

Wagner, Robert, 103, 104
Wallace, Henry, 122
Wall Street Journal, The, 38–39
Weinstein, James, 58, 93
Williams, G. Mennen, 123, 132, 133, 140, 144, 145
Women's movement, 21, 43–44, 45
Woodcock, Leonard, 19, 141
Worker, The, 59, 73
World War I, 76–77
World War II, 48, 49

Young, Andrew, 34, 36
Young Socialist Alliance (YSA), 9, 63, 99

CAPITALIST CRISIS AND THE FIGHT FOR WORKERS POWER

Are They Rich Because They're Smart?
Class, Privilege, and Learning under Capitalism
JACK BARNES

Exposes growing class inequalities in the US and the self-serving rationalizations of well-paid professionals who think their "brilliance" equips them to "regulate" working people, who don't know what's in their own best interest. $10. Also in Spanish, French, Farsi, and Arabic.

The Clintons' Anti-Working-Class Record
Why Washington Fears Working People
JACK BARNES

What working people need to know about the profit-driven course of Democrats and Republicans alike over the last thirty years. And the political awakening of workers seeking to understand and resist the capitalist rulers' assaults. $10. Also in Spanish, French, Farsi, and Greek.

The Transitional Program for Socialist Revolution
LEON TROTSKY

The Socialist Workers Party program, drafted by Trotsky in 1938, still guides the SWP and communists the world over. The party "uncompromisingly gives battle to all political groupings tied to the apron strings of the bourgeoisie. Its task—the abolition of capitalism's domination. Its aim—socialism. Its method—the proletarian revolution." $17. Also in Farsi.

In Defense of the US Working Class
MARY-ALICE WATERS

"Without understanding the devastation of the lives of working-class families in the US, you can't understand what's happening in politics." When tens of thousands of West Virginia teachers and school employees set an example in 2018 with their victorious strikes, they drew on the fighting traditions of oppressed and exploited producers of all skin colors and national origins. They fought for dignity and respect for themselves, their families, and for all working people. $7. Also in Spanish, French, Farsi, and Greek.

Is Socialist Revolution in the US Possible?
A Necessary Debate among Working People
MARY-ALICE WATERS

Fighting for a society only working people can create, it is our own capacities we will discover. And along that course we will answer the question posed here with a resounding "Yes." Possible but not inevitable. That depends on us. $7. Also in Spanish, French, and Farsi.

"It's the Poor Who Face the Savagery of the US 'Justice' System"
The Cuban Five Talk about Their Lives within the US Working Class

How US cops, courts, and prisons work as "an enormous machine for grinding people up." Five Cuban revolutionaries framed up and held in US jails for 16 years explain the human devastation of capitalist "justice"—and how socialist Cuba is different. $10. Also in Spanish, Farsi, and Greek.

WWW.PATHFINDERPRESS.COM

EXPAND YOUR REVOLUTIONARY LIBRARY

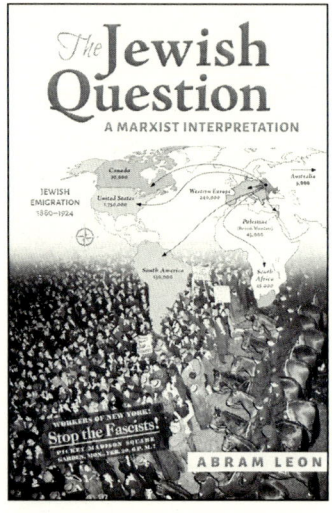

The Jewish Question
A Marxist Interpretation
ABRAM LEON

Why is Jew-hatred still raising its ugly head? What are its class roots—from antiquity through feudalism, to capitalism's rise and current crises? Why is there no solution under capitalism without revolutionary struggles that transform working people as we fight to transform our world? The author, Abram Leon, was killed in the Nazi gas chambers. This 2020 edition has a revised translation, new introduction, and 40 pages of illustrations and maps. $17. Also in Spanish and French.

Che Guevara Talks to Young People

Guevara challenges the youth of Cuba and the world to work. To become disciplined. To join the vanguard on the front lines of struggles, small and large. To become a different kind of human being as they fight together with working people of all lands to transform the world. $12. Also in Spanish and Greek.

The Rise and Fall of the Nicaraguan Revolution

Based on ten years of socialist journalism from inside Nicaragua, this special issue of *New International* recounts the achievements and worldwide impact of the 1979 Nicaraguan revolution. It traces the political retreat of the Sandinista National Liberation Front leadership that led to the downfall of the workers and farmers government in the closing years of the 1980s. Documents of the Socialist Workers Party by Jack Barnes, Steve Clark, and Larry Seigle. In *New International* no. 9. $14. Also in Spanish.

Teamster Rebellion
FARRELL DOBBS

The 1934 strikes that won union recognition for truckers and warehouse workers in Minneapolis and helped pave the way for the working-class social movement that built the industrial unions. The first of four volumes by a central leader of these battles. $16. Also in Spanish, French, Farsi, and Greek.

The History of the Russian Revolution
LEON TROTSKY

How, under Lenin's leadership, the Bolshevik Party led millions of workers and farmers to overthrow the state power of the landlords and capitalists in 1917 and bring to power a government that advanced their class interests at home and worldwide. Unabridged, 3 vols. in one. Written by one of the central leaders of that socialist revolution. $30. Also in French and Russian.

Maurice Bishop Speaks
The Grenada Revolution and Its Overthrow, 1979–83

The triumph of the 1979 revolution in the Caribbean island of Grenada under the leadership of Maurice Bishop gave hope to millions throughout the Americas. Invaluable lessons from the workers and farmers government destroyed by a Stalinist-led counterrevolution in 1983. $20

WWW.PATHFINDERPRESS.COM

February 1965: The Final Speeches
MALCOLM X

Our revolt is not "simply a racial conflict of Black against white, or a purely American problem. Rather, we are seeing a global rebellion of the oppressed against the oppressor, the exploited against the exploiter." Speeches and interviews from the last three weeks of Malcolm X's life. $17

50 Years of Covert Operations in the US
Washington's Political Police and the American Working Class
LARRY SEIGLE, FARRELL DOBBS, STEVE CLARK

How class-conscious workers have fought against the drive to build the "national security" state essential to maintaining capitalist rule. $10. Also in Spanish and Farsi.

Genocide against the Indians
GEORGE NOVACK

Why did the leaders of the Europeans who settled in North America try to exterminate the peoples already living there? How was the campaign of genocide against the Indians linked to the expansion of capitalism in the United States? Noted Marxist George Novack answers these questions. $5. Also in Farsi.

The Communist Manifesto
KARL MARX AND
FREDERICK ENGELS

Communism, say the founding leaders of the revolutionary workers movement, is not a set of ideas or preconceived "principles" but workers' line of march to power, springing from a "movement going on under our very eyes." $5. Also in Spanish, French, Farsi, and Arabic.

Feminism and the Marxist Movement
MARY-ALICE WATERS

Since the founding of the modern revolutionary workers movement nearly 150 years ago, Marxists have championed the struggle for women's rights and explained the economic roots in class society of women's oppression. "The struggle for women's liberation," Waters writes, "was lifted out of the realm of the personal, the 'impossible dream,' and unbreakably linked to the progressive forces of our epoch"—the working-class struggle for power. $5. Also in Farsi.

Thomas Sankara Speaks
The Burkina Faso Revolution,
1983–87

Under Sankara's guidance, Burkina Faso's revolutionary government led peasants, workers, women, and youth to expand literacy; to sink wells, plant trees, erect housing; to combat women's oppression; to carry out land reform; to join others in Africa and worldwide to free themselves from the imperialist yoke. $20. Also in French.

WWW.PATHFINDERPRESS.COM

CUBA'S SOCIALIST REVOLUTION

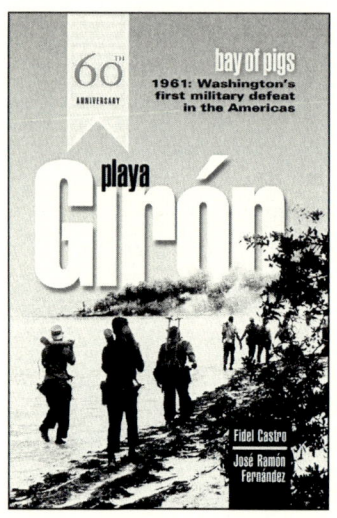

Playa Girón/Bay of Pigs
Washington's First Military Defeat in the Americas
FIDEL CASTRO, JOSÉ RAMÓN FERNÁNDEZ

In fewer than 72 hours of combat in April 1961, Cuba's revolutionary armed forces defeated a US-organized invasion by 1,500 mercenaries. In the process, the Cuban people set an example for workers, farmers, and youth the world over that with political consciousness, class solidarity, courage, and revolutionary leadership, one can stand up to enormous might and seemingly insurmountable odds—and win. $17. Also in Spanish.

Women in Cuba: The Making of a Revolution Within the Revolution
VILMA ESPÍN, ASELA DE LOS SANTOS, YOLANDA FERRER

The integration of women into the ranks and leadership of the Cuban Revolution was inseparable from its working-class course from the start. This is the story of that revolution and how it transformed the women and men who made it. $17. Also in Spanish and Greek.

The First and Second Declarations of Havana

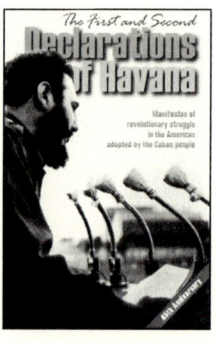

Nowhere are the questions of revolutionary strategy that today confront men and women on the front lines of struggles in the Americas addressed with greater truthfulness and clarity than in these uncompromising indictments of imperialist plunder and "the exploitation of man by man." Adopted by million-strong assemblies of the Cuban people in 1960 and 1962. $10. Also in Spanish, French, Farsi, Arabic, and Greek.

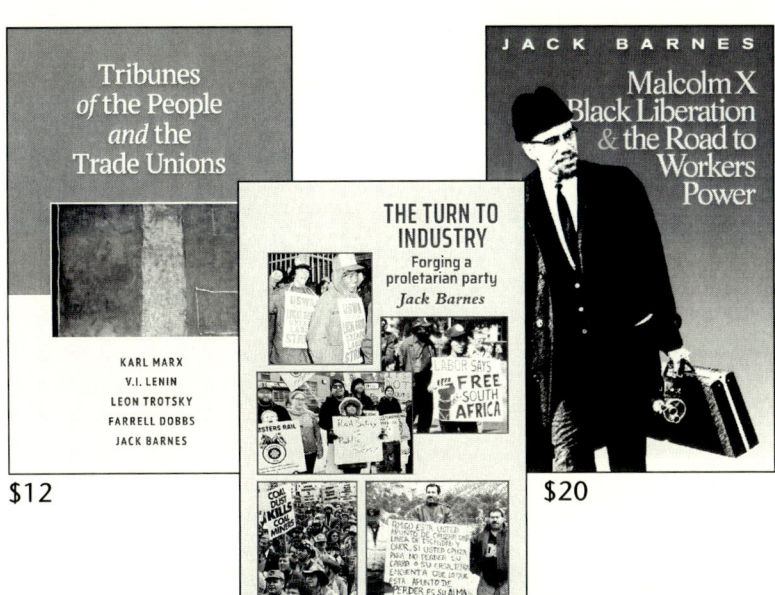

$12 $20

$15

Three books to be read as one ...

... about building the only kind of party worthy of the name "revolutionary" in the imperialist epoch.

- A party that's working class in program, composition, and action.
- A party that recognizes, in word and deed, the most revolutionary fact of our time:

  That working people—those the bosses and privileged layers who serve them fear as "deplorables," "criminals," or just plain "trash"—have the power to create a different world as we organize and act together to defend our own interests, not those of the class that grows rich off exploiting our labor. That as we advance along that revolutionary course, we'll transform ourselves and awaken to our capacities—to our own worth.

Three books about building such a party in the US and throughout the capitalist world. Also in Spanish and French.

Special Offer!
All three $30

The Turn to Industry and *Tribunes of the People and the Trade Unions* $20

Either book plus *Malcolm X, Black Liberation, and the Road to Workers Power* $25

WWW.PATHFINDERPRESS.COM

ALSO FROM PATHFINDER

Cuba and the Coming American Revolution
JACK BARNES

This is a book about the struggles of working people in the imperialist heartland, the youth attracted to them, and the example set by the Cuban people that revolution is not only necessary—it can be made. It is about the class struggle in the US, where the revolutionary capacities of workers and farmers are today as utterly discounted by the ruling powers as were those of the Cuban toilers. And just as wrongly. $10. Also in Spanish, French, and Farsi.

Red Zone
Cuba and the Battle against Ebola in West Africa
ENRIQUE UBIETA GÓMEZ

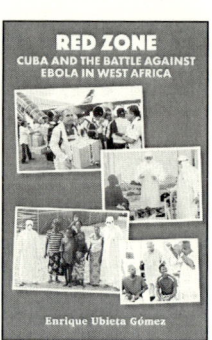

When three African countries were hit in 2014–15 by the largest Ebola epidemic on record, Cuba's revolutionary government responded to an international call and sent what no other country even pretended to provide: more than 250 volunteer doctors, nurses, and other medical workers. This firsthand account of their actions shows the kind of men and women only a socialist revolution can produce. $17. Also in Spanish and French.

Socialism on Trial
Testimony at Minneapolis Sedition Trial
JAMES P. CANNON

The revolutionary program of the working class, presented in response to frame-up charges of "seditious conspiracy" in 1941, on the eve of US entry into World War II. The defendants were leaders of the Minneapolis labor movement and the Socialist Workers Party. $15. Also in Spanish, French, and Farsi.

Cosmetics, Fashions, and the Exploitation of Women
JOSEPH HANSEN, EVELYN REED, MARY-ALICE WATERS

How big business reinforces women's second-class status and uses it to rake in profits. Where does women's oppression come from? How has the entry of millions of women into the workforce strengthened the battle for emancipation, still to be won? $12. Also in Spanish, Farsi, and Greek.

Fascism: What It Is and How to Fight It
LEON TROTSKY

Writing in the heat of struggle against the rising fascist movement in Europe in the 1930s, Russian communist leader Leon Trotsky examines the origins and nature of fascism and advances, for the first time, a working-class strategy to combat and defeat it. $5. Also in French.

Puerto Rico: Independence Is a Necessity
RAFAEL CANCEL MIRANDA

One of the five Puerto Rican Nationalists imprisoned by Washington for more than 25 years and released in 1979 speaks out on the brutal reality of US colonial domination, the example of Cuba's socialist revolution, and the ongoing struggle for independence. $5. Also in Spanish and Farsi.

WWW.PATHFINDERPRESS.COM

PATHFINDER AROUND THE WORLD

UNITED STATES
(and Caribbean, Latin America, and East Asia)
Pathfinder Books, 306 W. 37th St., 13th Floor
New York, NY 10018

CANADA
Pathfinder Books, 7107 St. Denis, Suite 204
Montreal, QC H2S 2S5

UNITED KINGDOM
(and Europe, Africa, Middle East, and South Asia)
Pathfinder Books, 5 Norman Rd.
Seven Sisters, London N15 4ND

AUSTRALIA
(and Southeast Asia and the Pacific)
Pathfinder Books, Suite 103, 124-128 Beamish St.
Campsie, Sydney
Postal address: P.O. Box 73, Campsie, NSW 2194

NEW ZEALAND
Pathfinder Books, 188a Onehunga Mall Rd.
Onehunga, Auckland 1061
Postal address: P.O. Box 13857, Auckland 1643

pathfinderpress.com

Visit our website for all our titles, to place orders,
and to join the

PATHFINDER READERS CLUB
25% off all titles
30% off books of the month

JOIN NOW!
$10 a year

Valid at pathfinderpress.com
and local book centers